NO SEX PLEASE, WE'RE SINGLE

No Sex Please, We're Single

IAN STUART GREGORY

KINGSWAY PUBLICATIONS
EASTBOURNE

ISBN 0 85476 715 0

Co-published in South Africa with
SCB Publishers
Cornelis Struik House, 80 McKenzie Street
Cape Town 8001, South Africa.
Reg no 04/02203/06

Designed and produced by Bookprint Creative Services
P.O. Box 827, BN21 3YJ, England for
KINGSWAY PUBLICATIONS LTD
Lottbridge Drove, Eastbourne, East Sussex BN23 6NT.
Printed in Great Britain.

Contents

Author's Note

It is said that 'to have one source is plagiarism, to have two is research'. So to add a modicum of respectability to this book there follow details of where I stole most of my material from. Elaine Storkey's *The Search for Intimacy* (Hodder & Stoughton) is a fabulous read on relationships in general. The figures on pre-marital sex are quoted by her from the 1994 report 'Sexual Behaviour in Britain'. Patrick Dixon's *The Rising Price of Love* (Hodder & Stoughton) gathers together the evidence of the cost to society of family breakdown. The *Social Trends* survey highlighting the rise and rise of singleness is quoted from *The Guardian*, 1st February 1997. I'm indebted to Mark Surey of the Messianic Testimony for his insight into Jewish dating culture. Figures for the effect of pre-marital cohabitation on subsequent divorce rates vary between countries – Elaine Storkey quotes research of a 50% greater incidence of divorce for British couples who lived together before marrying. Finally, I thank the Revd Paul Dunthorne for guiding me through the Bible's views on pre-marital sex and *porneia*. If there is other research you are aware of which is relevant to this book's remit, then I would be grateful if you would drop me a line.

Preface
The Singles Scene

Most Christian singles, myself included, look forward to being married. Yet most of the books about us are written by people who are not having to deal with the issue first hand. That's because either they are already married, or they don't want to get married. Such books invariably seem focused on 'coping' with being single, not on examining why increasing numbers of Christians remain single despite wanting to be married. And rarely are they direct in dealing with our complex struggle of preserving and restoring emotional wholeness in the midst of a sexually anarchic society.

Involuntary singleness has never been easy. But what is different today is that in both the Christian community and society outside the number of unwilling solos is on the increase. More and more of our generation are staying single for longer, despite wanting to get married, which suggests that the process of finding a mate is becoming ever more difficult.

This book argues that rather than offering a remedy, most of our churches are failing spectacularly over relationship formation. Many of our leaders stay silent on the issue because they don't want to upset those who have decided not to marry. Others do speak out, but their perceptions are out of date – timewarped from a generation ago when courtship was utterly different from today. And a fair few are profoundly secular, preferring to leave it to the marriage 'market place' to operate, with a crossed-fingered hope that things will work out.

Some churches are wonderful: their singles don't feel pressurised into marriage by being patronised or treated as second-class citizens. They also have a vibrant social and spiritual life out of which many marriages are formed. But in so many other congregations there is a static, even stagnant, social scene. Singles who remain in such churches – and many don't – are confronted with a minimal, or non-existent, choice of partners. Marriages which do take place are often poor matches where the most significant area of compatibility was a sense of mutual desperation. Any surprise, then, that divorce has increased in the church?

Just as our churches differ, so do we. For while there are those singles for whom the longing to marry dominates their lives, others are much more optimistic about finding a partner, although they still find the whole business confusing. And then there are quite a few who have turbo-charged romantic lives. Unfortunately their relationships tend to veer off course when things go too fast.

In this book I offer practical ideas for all types of singles – as well as for church leaders – on how to improve the way relationships between Christians are formed. But while we singles are very motivated to deal with our personal situation, I am not optimistic that many ministers will respond to the challenge. For when things are so obviously wrong, too many church leaders do nothing because to do what is obviously needed is to admit that it should have been done before.

So in the middle section of this book it's back to us – the singles – as I try to unravel the spaghetti of confusion that messes up our romantic lives. The last section is devoted to where and how we can meet the people we desire, as well as who and when. I'm seeking both to find biblical principles about how single men and women should relate, and also to apply them to today's culture.

There is no greater focus of restlessness in Britain's churches than the army of single Christians who are struggling with being unmarried.

There is no greater wound haemorrhaging young people from the body of Christ than the defection of those who have given up on finding a Christian spouse. There is no greater source for secular contempt for the church than its image as a home for singles who are either sexual hypocrites or sexually repressed. From our clergy there is invariably silence on the struggle of being a single Christian in a sex-obsessed society. Silence born out of ignorance or embarrassment. And when singles aren't being

ignored, they are so often being patronised. To many
of our faithful singles there is the growing fear that
their church membership is becoming a life sentence
of sexual and emotional isolation. They see a receding prospect of finding a Christian spouse. To them
church is a celibacy club.

I thank all my single Christian friends for their
ideas and enthusiasm for this book. While I have
shamelessly stolen their thoughts, a few of mine
remain. I don't mind if you disagree with those, or
if you think that there are issues which I should have
covered. For above all, the purpose of this book is
simply to stir up an overdue debate among single
people about how we meet and how we conduct our
relationships. If we develop and apply a theology of
romance then our church can recover credibility both
with its own singles and with those in the world
outside. Send a copy of this book to your pastor so
that maybe he or she also will be challenged to think
about the issues afresh. And please do let me know
your thoughts . . . so that a second edition can be
your book.

SECTION ONE
Singleness and the Church

1
Navigating the
Post-Marriage Society

Forty years ago there was a great way of avoiding the temptations of pre-marital sex. People got married — typically in their early twenties. Mind you, they weren't perfect: a little under half of the women were virgins on their wedding night, and only about 14 per cent of their husbands. But that's still a lot better than our generation is managing today: 4 per cent for women, 1 per cent for men. Not much scope for more failure here!

In our parents' day the accepted wisdom from friends, teachers and the media was that sex should be saved until the wedding night. Nowadays avoiding pre-marital sex is seen as unrealistic. Perversely society sees our self-control as dysfunctional, not virtuous.

The norm in our culture now is to postpone marriage to allow careers to develop and, where folk do get hitched, to see it as a commitment made not until death do them part, but until one of them is fed up. Many skip it altogether for casual relationships and all too many have simply lost count of the number of sexual partners they have had. In the 1990s cohabitation, not marriage, is the step of commitment our secular friends worry about.

Not such a liberated generation when we look at the results that shackle people today. Children raised without a stable relationship between their parents are less able to form stable friendships as adults. The more hurt people are the less they are able to trust, and without trust there can be no relationships. The decline in relationships has become a vicious downward spiral. Every now and then our politicians look at the price tag of immorality and decide it is costing a bit too much in terms of single-parent families, crime and indiscipline. They see the problems, but they do not have a solution.

And if the past is not so hot, the future is positively scary. The British government's Social Trends Survey projects that by the year 2020 one in three people won't just be single, but also living on their own. *The Guardian* newspaper wonders whether we will 'fragment into two nations; the smug couples and the bitter singles'. In this brave new Britain, *The Guardian* argues, there could be '10 million people who might like to come home to somebody else. Each other perhaps. Clearly, there is some kind of communication breakdown going on.' Across all age ranges, from young-never-marrieds to elderly widows, involuntary singleness is a national disease that is out of control. They know that committed relationships are far from easy to sustain, that getting married is no guarantee of happiness, but they still want someone to come home to.

What an opportunity for our churches! For as our

society slides, we have the opportunity to become each community's alternative culture that shines in the midst of the darkness; a sanctuary from that darkness, where stable relationships are formed and nurtured, and where morality is not only taught but seen to work.

> **While revival is a sovereign work of God, there is a tremendous amount of 'natural' growth available to churches which look after their singles well.**

But to date we seem to be missing our big chance, because far from offering an alternative to the world, our churches simply seem to be tracking the world. Figures from the UK Evangelical Alliance show that 35 per cent of adults in evangelical churches are unmarried – and the trend is upwards. Our churches are becoming singles clubs where people don't get paired off.

This is because three huge post-war trends are making it more difficult for Christian singles to form lasting relationships. First, the rise in individualism has not only made people more shy of commitment, but it has also shredded the community structures through which so many of our parents met each other. Secondly, there is the social earthquake caused by the invention of the pill and the rise of feminism. Regardless of whether we consider feminism to be broadly positive or negative, we cannot deny that it has radically changed relationships between the sexes. The ways men and women relate to each other have still to adjust fully to this shift in power and expectations. And thirdly, the decline in the size of the church has meant that we Christians fish in smaller ponds in which there is less chance of a suitable 'catch'.

The combined effect of these trends is seen in the dramatic rise in involuntary singleness which is not simply the result of there being more women in the church than men. Such undesired singleness creates confusion and frustration – the breeding grounds for defection. Throughout my Christian life – as a teenager, at university, in my twenties and now in my early thirties – I have seen so many people fall away from their faith because of dating non-Christians that it amounts to a slow-motion crisis for the church. These are Christians who, while believing that marrying a compatible believer was preferable, had lost hope in this Christian ideal happening for them and decided to settle for a tangible, available relationship. The challenge for the church is to give those tempted to leave reasons to hope. Partly this is a matter of encouraging them to see that their relationship with God is much more important than any human relationship. But we also have to look for practical ways of improving their chances of finding a suitable Christian.

It may be only a minority who are this depressed about being single. But among other singles there is still enough confusion and unease both to offend our pastoral hearts and to disturb our evangelical minds. For an unhappy church is not going to grow. Nor is

God likely to visit an immoral church with revival. We, the church, acknowledge that God has created us as social beings who want to relate to each other, yet what are we doing to deal with the social needs of our singles?

Creating healthy male–female relationships should be an area that we Christians are good at. After all, our God invented marriage. Living godly lives as single people and seeking a marriage partner are supremely important issues for the church as a whole, as well as being crucial to you and me as individuals. Yet in the church and in society outside, more and more of our generation are staying single for longer, despite wanting to get married, and this suggests that the process of finding a partner is becoming increasingly difficult. In the church this rise in involuntary singleness has led to more frustration, more immorality and more bad matches being formed. None of which makes the church attractive to non-Christians, or helps it retain the singles it has. Yet despite all this, too many married Christians seem indifferent or patronising towards single people searching for a partner, and so many church leaders, who may otherwise be greatly respected, appear to have a blind spot when it comes to the process by which their unmarrieds might get paired off.

One day, like Rip Van Winkle, our leaders are going to wake up to see how much the singles scene has changed since their day – the huge seismic shifts in the way Christian men and women interact. Our leaders need to spot the rapidly rising number of singles in their churches and society as a whole, and start to regard us not as a pastoral irritant but as an engine of growth. This group not only needs to have more input if it is to thrive, but it is facing such a fast-changing social situation that it needs radical new wisdom; wisdom which understands both our national culture and our Christian sub-culture and comes up with fresh ideas on how to make the covenant with God relevant to today's singles.

Isn't that what wisdom is – making the covenant between God and man relevant to each generation's circumstances; the application of biblical principles to today's culture, not the culture of forty years ago or even two thousand years ago? We need to extract the biblical principles of purity, pledging troth, and self-control, and learn how to teach them to a culture that sees these words as foreign remnants of a dead language. In the next chapter I show how the rewards are clear for those churches which do this for their own singles. They have a happier group of singles who don't feel trapped in being unmarried. If the Christian singles scene in your church becomes more vibrant then it will also become more attractive to non-Christians tasting your church to see if it does offer a better life.

The central question I'm trying to explore in this book is why there are so many unmarrieds in the church. I know far too many eligible Christian men well into their thirties (and beyond) to believe that this is purely down to a 'man shortage' in the church. These are men who, like the women they sit near in church, long to marry. Yet it doesn't seem to happen. Why is that?

The second section deals with a lot of the 'ologies' that stop us from being married. I mean our dodgy theology and our dodgier still personal psychology. For good measure I'll drop in a bit of sociology and some of our 1990s ideology. Hold tight to your hang-ups, because I'm going to give them a good kick!

It will probably come as no big shock that this book on singleness also discusses the super-sensitive topic of pre-marital sex. Most of us are well aware of how destructive it can be in undermining relationships – we just try to delude ourselves occasionally that it is not. There are plenty of hot potatoes and I hope that I have not missed any of the areas of sexuality which are important to you.

Most of us have a theology of romance that owes more to Mills and Boon novels than it does to the Bible.

The sex stuff will no doubt be well thumbed through, but the chapter which I think will be most challenging is the one on 'quitting fantasyland'. That's because most of us have a theology of romance that owes more to Mills and Boon novels than it does to the Bible. If we are not rigorous in discarding cherished notions which are not valid from the point of view of either reason or Scripture, then our chances of finding a good marriage partner are much reduced.

Having hopefully both encouraged and challenged you, the last section of the book addresses our Christian dating culture. First and foremost, I'm going to ask you to ask yourself what it is you are looking for. Are these qualities the essential ones which make a good marriage, or are they peripherals?

Another tough issue is when we should start seriously looking for a partner. Then there is the issue of how and where we meet. If you are not meeting enough eligible Christians in your own church where else should you look? And how should you go about approaching those people you would like to know better? Not wanting to be seen showing an interest in someone, we often prefer to risk missing out on meeting someone rather than being rejected, or, worse still, being labelled as 'desperate'. Too many Christians are at the polar extreme of the confident, relaxed approach to dating where two people think nothing of going out with each other for a meal and it being left as that — a good evening out with no expectations on either side. In our church culture one of the parties would feel rejected as potential marriage material and would be even less willing to risk further self-perceived rejection by either asking someone else out or agreeing to a date in the future. Rather we inwardly moan about the difficulties of relationships. We suffer in silence, saying that everything is 'fine' when it patently isn't. We do not have the courage to take a risk.

Some definitions

One of the problems of discussing the ways men and women form relationships is that words such as 'dating' mean different things to different people. There's no right or wrong meaning, but for the purposes of this book I will use the phrase 'going out' to mean an exclusive relationship where two people are evaluating each other as potential marriage partners, and probably spending a fair bit of time hugging and kissing. I will use 'dating' to describe men and women seeing each other to work out if their friendship might grow into romance but without it being exclusive or in any way physical. 'Being friends' refers to two people who enjoy seeing each other but who are both content that their friendship is not going to become a romance.

2
The Pastoral Impact

It always amazes me how Christians can be so short-sighted about church growth. I mean they can be fine about evangelism – preaching the gospel, holding missions and the like – but they don't consider whether or not beyond the number of conversions their church is actually growing. The total attending a church is a product not only of the numbers coming into the faith, but also the result of people leaving. Now since we naturally like to focus on success it is not surprising that the people who do the counting are much better at trumpeting the arrivals than the departures. In any case, we hope against hope that those who have left are only 'temporarily absent' and since they are by definition not coming to church they are difficult to track down.

My experience of seventeen years of church life is that those who wander away are predominantly singles. It may in part be because they lack the encouragement of a believing spouse to prod them to go to church when they're not in the mood, and singles much more than couples can be absent from church for weeks before anyone in the congregation notices. But perhaps the key difference is that singles face a greater tension than couples between the standards of their secular friends and the Christian lifestyle. While married couples are respected by the world for remaining faithful, Christian singles are often derided for staying celibate – not least if this has been their way of life for years. But however hurtful being mocked by the world is, Christian singles find the words of fellow believers more painful still.

Ten Unhelpful Things Married Couples Say to Singles

1. You'll meet someone when you least expect it.

2. God's got just the right person waiting for you.

3. I'm so grateful that God gave me my partner.

4. Why don't you pray about it?

5. How wonderful that you have so much spare time.

6. You're lucky not to have children – they're such hard work.

7. Would you like to help with the crèche?

8. I don't know how I would have coped if I was still single.

9. Why didn't you get married to the person you were seeing last year?

10. You can't afford to be too choosy.

If only these mindless banalities weren't being said around this nation's churches! For Christian singles don't just leave church because they feel pulled by the world, but because they also feel pushed by fellow believers. While many singles laugh off such thoughtless words, they cause deep wounds for those who are sensitive about being unmarried. (We get enough subtle hints from our family without needing them at church as well.)

The question is, why do married couples resort to these platitudes when talking to singles? Is it that they don't understand or respect singles? Is it that these stock phrases are a means of avoiding having to offer practical help or encouragement to a single person? Or is that they just love to gossip?

The tasks single people are offered in a church communicate underlying attitudes as much as words. When single people marry they can suddenly find themselves being given higher profile responsibilities within a church, the added respect purely a function of their having 'arrived' in the married world.

It's this higher status given to the married that intensifies the pressures to escape from singleness. A common feature of churches that have contented singles is that they have systematically gone through their language and attitudes to purge themselves of anything that suggests marriage is superior to singlenesss. They take it seriously that such hierarchical views are unbiblical and a reverse of earlier church practice in which singleness was deemed more respectable. Churches that don't examine themselves become two communities: singles and marrieds.

No hope

As well as pressures from the world and pressures from married believers, Christian singles also have to deal with the pressures within themselves. How should involuntary singles cope with the soul-sapping despair that their singleness has no horizon but death? As their thirties head towards their forties, the prospect looms of becoming a 'never will marry'. What is a woman to do if she longs to be a mother yet is seeing her child-bearing years slipping away with no eligible men in her church? Wait for an Abraham? Or start a relationship with an available non-Christian? Spare a thought too for the older bachelors in the church – often bachelors because they are short on social skills. Their cause is not helped by their advancing years.

Not everyone fits in with the depressing caricature painted above. A lot of Christians are relaxed about being single, confident that the right person will turn up. But many readers will recognise the description of depressed, despairing single Christians as reflecting truths about large swathes of the church.

It matters, not only because Christ is not honoured by a church which allows so many of its young people to flounder on such a crucial issue, but also because far too many previously faithful followers fall away from church at this hurdle. This may be through a short-term temptation: an opportunity for physical intimacy is hard to turn down for those to whom the church offers only an unleavened diet of sexual restraint. Such moral failure leaves many feeling out of place in God's holy house. And even if they find Christ's ready forgiveness, their fellow Christians are not always as forgiving as God.

Tough on sin, tough on the causes of sin

This is not a call for tolerance of sexual sin. It is a plea for sympathy for our singles. A sympathy not limited to words but one that goes the second mile in offering practical help to the Christian unmarried in their search for a partner and support in their intervening angst. The stress for involuntary singles comes when they cannot see opportunities for meeting eligible Christians. If church leaders and Christian married couples stopped sweeping the problem under the carpet but addressed it with both words and deeds, then singles would not feel so trapped. It is talking openly about the issue and being very practical that helps singles get marriage into perspective. If no one appears to be listening to a single person's concerns, then their worries are amplified as they echo inside their head. For too long the attitude among church leaders has been that talking about the issue will simply fuel the angst, but this is not so. Talk about our worries and we feel understood. Help us practically and we feel cared for.

However large the flow of singles is out of church, the principal cause of it is the very pressure of being single. So strong is the desire among many to share the emotional and physical companionship of a partner that if the church does not hold out a realistic prospect of marriage to us single Christians, then we will be prone to stray. Most of us are willing to avoid pre-marital sex and instead channel our sexual drive towards marriage. But the longer that pipeline becomes the harder it becomes. If years of being part of the Christian community have failed to produce any prospect of a marriage partner, then hope begins to die and despair drives people from the church.

> **For church leaders to ignore the matching process is not only pastorally bad practice, it is also a strategic blunder hindering the cause of church growth.**

Just how many singles leave the church on this issue is all but impossible to quantify. Even if opinion polls were to be conducted, few would be willing to admit to quitting faith over this failure to find a spouse. But the anecdotal evidence and logic do point us in this direction that sexual attraction does have a powerful influence on church attendance. As a thirteen-year-old I recall becoming increasingly aware of the girls at the back of the church. It was a few years before I met up with God, but I know what the attraction was! A similar tale is told by a professional friend who left church in her early twenties because she could not find a boyfriend, and then returned to the fold several years later because 'there was a chap I fancied'.

The purists may 'tut-tut' about this and say that

the only motivation for coming to church should be a desire to know God, but such 'spiritual' arguments are neither realistic nor godly. They are unrealistic because only someone with blinkers could fail to realise how strong a motivation the desire for a sexual partner and emotional companion is in our society. They are ungodly because this very desire is placed in our hearts by our Creator who not only said that it is not right for man to be alone, but also provided a partner for Adam.

If we want churches where singles have their eyes focused upwards worshipping God rather than sideways eyeing up the talent, then we must deal with these concerns. It is only when singles regard themselves as having a strong chance of finding a good marriage partner that they will be able to forget about the issue and 'let it happen'. It is only when they are relaxed about their marriage prospects that they will be able to see that marriage is not the only source of companionship; that being single is a time in which to rejoice and make great lifelong friendships. It is only when single people are confident of being able to marry that they stop treating being single as merely a waiting room for marriage.

Some will dismiss what I am arguing by saying that the logical conclusion is that churches should organise dating agencies. Well, why not? Many of their members would stay if they did! Whether or not the response is that extreme, what I am urging is that there must be a response rather than ecclesiastical handwashing and wringing. Where there is a problem in the community in that people's God-given desire for partners is not being satisfied, then there is also a God-given responsibility on the church community to address the issue.

You may say, 'Where in the Bible does it say that church leaders should facilitate marriages?' But I would ask in reply, 'Where in the Bible does it say that churches should have car parks?' Yet many ministers, seeing that the congregation can't get to worship because they can't park their cars, will seek to provide a practical answer without resorting to biblical precedent. So equally, where there is this serious problem of single people finding it difficult to find partners, why not address it practically as well? Setting up a dating agency or offering arranged marriages may not be culturally appropriate, but we must then find something that will work in our culture.

A few will seek refuge from action by overspiritualising the matter, saying, 'If God wants them to marry he will provide partners.' Others in Thatcherite tradition will comfort themselves that 'these things are best left for the market to sort out'. But this *laissez-faire* approach to marriage is in variance to the practice of the other major faiths. Think of the Jewish, Muslim, Hindu and Sikh religions. They would not dream of allowing their young, their future, to drift away from their communities because they could not find a partner within the faith. They will not only go the second mile to help form relationships within the faith, they will go thousands of miles – across continents – to find a faith match. Now if this is what other faiths do for those who are reluctant to remain, is it not incumbent upon the Christian family to think of what help they could offer to those who are so very keen to stay within the fold?

A first practical response from our churches could be to think through the implications of the demands they place on their unmarrieds. First, they are telling them not to consider marrying 97 per cent of the available members of the opposite sex. This is sound advice as there is no better way to be dragged from your faith than being locked into a marriage with an unbeliever. But the result of this is that many of the main routes to relationships for non-Christians are not available to believers. For instance, in the United States some 90 per cent of professional couples meet each other at work. Now for Christian professionals in Britain, on average 97 per cent of their colleagues won't be believers. Nor will the person you bump into on the train (how my parents met) or meet at a dance class (how my sister met her husband) be at all likely to be a Christian. The net effect is that it puts an immense amount of pressure on single Christians to meet each other at the only place where most people are believers – their churches.

But these pools in which Christian singles fish have shrunk as Western Christianity has declined in the post-war period. Combine the impact of the shrinking percentage of Christians on the national and local level with endemic marriagephobia (by this I mean fear of not getting married as well as fear of being married), then you start to see how single Christians find it so very hard to find a good match.

Those very clever Jews

The remarkable survival of the Jewish people over
the millennia may owe just a little to the sophisti-
cated process of creating marriages. Jews living in
small communities (especially after the Diaspora)
had to come up with an efficient system of making
sure that its young were able to find the best available partners. The method that evolved was the
matchmaker couple – a husband and wife – who
acted as conduits of information. Let's look at the
system in theory. If a single young man, Dan, fancied Abigail, then he would let it be known to the
matchmaker husband. His wife, when sounding out
the women, would find that while Abigail did not
fancy Dan, Beth did. The advantage to Dan is that
he does not face the ordeal of being rejected by
Abigail. Instead he knows that if he is interested
Beth would like to know him better. The process
also empowers women. Apart from Abigail being
spared the embarrassment of having to turn down
Dan to his face, Beth has been able to express an
interest in Dan that she would never have felt able
to do directly.

Without requiring any coercion whatsoever, the
genius of the system is that it provides near perfect
information – and with it marriages which have
much better prospects. Compare this to today's modern Western society where the fear of rejection im-
prisons people in singleness. People remain single for
years, oblivious to the fact that there are many
people whom they like who are interested in them.

No one has the courage to make a move because all are fearful of being labelled desperate.

Of course a matchmaking system can be abused. Very close to where I live a Sikh man came under immense family pressure to end a relationship with a Muslim woman. They provided a number of Sikh women for him to meet, and with a heavy heart he decided to marry one of them. Now, after just a year, the barely consummated marriage has failed. He still feels passionately for the Muslim woman, yet she, feeling utterly rejected, won't allow him near her. If it's not coercion, then gossip can disable the process.

Let us not think, however, that matchmaking is something which is alien to our Christian faith, because for many hundreds of years – up to the seventeenth and eighteenth centuries – this was the normal way marriages were made. Up to that time, if I was a peasant believer then I would be seeking an older wife – older because she would probably be not only sturdy enough to help in the fields, but also unlikely to bear too many children whom I could not afford to feed. If I was from the nobility, then the pressure would be to have a younger wife, as that would maximise my chances of having a surviving heir to pass my estate on to.

Two developments undermined this process. The first was the growth of the middle classes, which didn't have the same pressures to produce a certain number of children so could risk 'love matches'. The second was the Enlightenment, which stressed the role of the individual and applauded romance. So the decline of arranged marriages was not prompted by spiritual judgement but social issues. Perhaps with our culture having changed so rapidly over the past few decades, processes like matchmaking might be worth reconsidering?

Or perhaps another approach. For while the growth of individualism has made Jewish youth more resistant to the use of matchmakers, their parents and religious leaders have simply changed tactics. In London's main Jewish district of Golders Green a huge effort goes into arranging social events for their young. Determined to defend both their faith and their culture from being eroded by marrying out, the principle is that events like discos for Jewish teenagers must be at least as good as their Gentile equivalent. The thirteen- to eighteen-year-old age group is particularly well served so that by the time they reach their twenties they have a well-formed network of Jewish friends from which to choose a partner. Their sense of community has also been deeply rooted and with that a desire to stay within it through their choice in marriage.

Many faith groups concentrate on arranging regular meetings with 'potentials'. They ensure that their sons and daughters have a different prospect round for supper each weekend. Again, it's not requiring a matchmaker to act as a go-between, rather it's simply providing additional choice of candidates with the right qualification – namely sharing the faith. Obviously such facilitation can also be abused by undue pressure, but where the free choice of unmarried people is respected, many singles would appreciate being given more potential partners from their community to choose from. Western free choice is meaningless if there is no one to choose.

If there is a lack of suitable volunteers for the role of matchmaker and not enough couples willing to host weekly dinner parties, what else might the church do to give its young real choice? A number of churches arrange weekly or monthly social meetings which aim to get singles to meet more people in both their own church and neighbouring congregations.

Unfortunately a lot of these ventures fail because, to put it bluntly, they get taken over by the socially dysfunctional, whose deep insecurity drives others away. Now here is a real dilemma, for how can we lock out of Christian gatherings some of our most needy brothers and sisters in Christ? But at the same time you and I know that their very neediness makes them offputting, as they constantly try to draw attention to themselves and demand more time than people are willing or able to give. So do we allow them to attend, even if that will sooner or later cause these social gatherings to fail?

Our usual response is to duck the issue. Yes, we want more social gatherings for singles and no, we don't want to exclude anyone – that wouldn't be politically correct. So what do we do? We are dishonest. Instead of holding church social events from which we feel we can't exclude anyone, we instead organise private gatherings from which we keep out the undesirable. We all know exactly who we won't invite to our parties, our cinema trips and our out-

ings because their company is offputting. So while
the needy get more needy – left on their own – our
consciences are clear that we are not excluding anyone from a church gathering.

So what should we do? First, to avoid going on a
guilt trip we need to recognise the difference between
friendship and fellowship. Fellowship is something
you and I should offer to all believers: the helping
hand to anyone in need. Friendship, on the other
hand, is a much more intimate relationship. Its very
intimacy means that we cannot have that many
friends. And, unlike fellowship, it is also a two-way
relationship in which both parties derive strength
from each other. Indeed, it is friendship, not
fellowship, that offers the foundation for marriage.

So friendship by its very nature does exclude. If we
want to foster more friendships in our churches, then
some exclusion will go on. But our duty of fellowship
demands that to those we exclude we offer alterna-
tives that are at least as good in terms of intimacy.
The aim is to build them up to the point whereby
they are able to make lasting friendships rather than
relationships based purely on their own needs. We
should exclude such deeply needy people from events
where they put people off, not simply because their
presence undermines these meetings, but because
their attendance harms the inadequate themselves
as they get cold-shouldered. Such ruthless compassion may not be in vogue, but is it more caring than
the way you operate? If our goal is to foster more
friendships out of which marriages will grow, we
must be radical enough to focus on the target.

The next question is, who will organise these events? I realise that for busy pastors, even if they are able delegators, the organisation of a social as well as a spiritual dimension poses an extra burden. But two points: first, the social side of church life is just as much on the heart of God as hymns and sermons. How can an unhappy people worship God? Secondly, just as a starving man cannot hear the gospel clearly when his belly rumbles so loudly, so also until the social hunger of the single is satisfied they will not be able to function well in church life. Ignoring the problem is hardly efficient when it risks not only losing the hard-earned gains of evangelism out of the back door, but also results in those who stay being perennially discontent.

A church where its single population is depleted by weddings rather than defections is a happier one, with fewer pastoral cases overloading clergy.

Is it not the heart of God to meet the deep yearnings of the single? Is it not the work of God for ministers to use their contacts to encourage the birth of Christian marriages? Is it not the mind of God to use our imagination to create new ways for Christian singles to meet, so that they might not be led into temptation?

Now here is the very good news: a rash of marriages tends to have a stabilising effect on a congregation. The phrase 'settling down' conveys that after getting married people tend to put down roots and become less transient. More married couples also means that there are more islands of hospitality in the church, and this provides visual confirmation to unmarried singles that their church is a living, dynamic, reproducing organism.

One immediate obstacle to the creation of more marriages is that often there simply are not enough men to go round. Is this the fault of non-Christian men or the church? Whether it is the effeminate image of the clergy, the church's ambiguity towards homosexuality or the unwillingness of men to admit their need of God, something is wrong with either the image or the message of the church. Saving secular man is important, not only for his own salvation but for the health of our church body. We have to understand his thought patterns and fears, and meet them in Christ. We also need to be more inspired in dealing with the Christian men we have – for example, those who want to marry but are handicapped by social ineptness. How many pastors take time to discuss with such men not only the type of woman they should aim to marry, but also the social skills needed to win her over?

Even in the big city churches where the balance between men and women is not too off centre, there are great difficulties. The stakes in the marriage game are so high that no one is willing to make a mistake. While the secular world will take refuge in the half-way home of cohabitation, for the Christian it is all or nothing. This often makes the Christian dating scene much more uptight than the secular scene. It becomes akin to trench warfare in which the participants may not enjoy being stuck in their trenches, but they find that a lot safer than going over the top into the dating battlefield. The later chapters of this book look in detail at the complex factors which inhibit relations between Christian men and women. But for now let us make the point that it is extraordinary that we can have churches with predominantly young unmarried congregations that have more people on their divorce recovery programmes than on their marriage preparation courses.

So having discussed what pastors should be doing, what should they be saying? Well, let us start with what they should not be saying: nothing! It is incredible that in a society which is so utterly obsessed with sex, where the emotional carnage of licentiousness is so obviously shredding society, many churches fail to provide guidance. It is not as if the Bible fails to mention sex! But whether it is down to coyness, or a pandering to utilitarian psychology ('If it makes you feel good then it's OK'), there is a failure to preach absolute morality. And it is that orthodoxy that we single people want to hear. We are sick of the world's immorality. We know it does not work – often through bitter personal experience. And we want and need our church to teach the certainties of the centuries. Let's put it another way. If issues of sexuality and relationships are what single people are constantly agonising over – what we worry about when our brains are in neutral – then churches need to give regular and detailed guidance.

Let me be bold: we don't want to hear the vicar's views on 'saving the whale'. And if truth be told there are times when we are not so keen to hear yet another sermon on revival. What is often much more relevant to us is to know how we can grow in relationships. Only when the Christian life is fulfilling our most basic needs – giving us purpose, self-worth and strong friendships – will we have confidence to sell church to our friends as a place where their basic needs can be met.

The actions of the church give singles the impression that they are only regarded as fully mature and capable of responsibility once they are married.

Even where churches do address relationships it can leave us singles feeling unvalued. Sermons on marriage seem fine, but singleness is ghettoised into specialised seminars and talks. In these talks lip service is given to St Paul's teaching about the value of singles to the church. But the actions of the church give singles the impression that they are only regarded as fully mature and capable of responsibility once they are married.

The oft-repeated 'uniqueness' of being single – our ability to devote ourselves to the Lord's work – is often little more than an illusion. In reality too many are pouring huge amounts of energy into an often frantic search for a partner. How many times a week would you say the average single person thinks about being unmarried? As the writer Mike Mason explains about marriage: 'The decisive finality of vows was intended to free people so that they need not see their life's energies being drained away in endless courting rituals, in the constant hunger for sexual fulfilment, and in a continual search for meaningful relationships.'

The message that singles need to hear is not merely the narrow one of sexual discipline and purity. They need help in countering today's secular gospel of individualism and short-termism. Preaching morality, character and the establishment of community cuts across the world's attitude of 'I want it . . . and I want it now'. Sexual restraint understood in the context of these broader values comes across not as repressive but constructive. Relentless individualism and short-termism has destroyed so much of the reality of community known by our parents. For single people, long out of their parental home and without their own families, the breakdown of the wider community is painfully felt. In our numbing isolation we are dimly aware that there was once a better way. If isolation is one of the devil's goals, then he has succeeded brilliantly.

The pain of isolation is such that if singles hear, see and feel that within church they are a vital part of the community, then the attractions of the world will not glow so brightly. Many church leaders may think that is the message they do communicate, but it is not being heard. Instead the sub-messages come across: the way that on the agenda of prayer meetings the needs of the married drown out petitions for the unmarried; the tendency for a minister to espouse a theology experienced through the prism of his married life and not to draw upon metaphors about the single life; and, more subtlely, the way that a testimony about how a married couple were 'meant for each other' implies to singles that no one has been 'meant' for them.

Writing to a fairly 'wild' church in Corinth, the apostle Paul uses the metaphor of the church being like a human body in which every part is dependent on every other. Modern physiotherapy understands just how true this is: if my ankle is twisted, not only will the affected area be in pain, but the impact on my posture will ricochet through the rest of my body. Likewise with the singles in the church. When they are in pain, the equilibrium of the rest of the body of Christ is affected.

Bible Quiz for Evangelicals

Which of the following is the most important scripture?

(a) 'It is not good for the man to be alone' (Gen 2:18)

(b) 'Go and make disciples of all nations' (Mt 28:19)

(c) 'Take care of my sheep' (Jn 21:16)

Certainly the second one is the most quoted. But how can we fulfil the Great Commission when the church is drained by the exodus of those singles who have fallen in love with non-Christians; and when there is so much unhappiness and immorality among those who remain? No strategic vision for world evangelisation can succeed if the army of singles who will take the message abroad is demoralised.

Some will say that I am overstating my case. My challenge to you is to conduct a survey among the singles in your congregation to find out their real views on singleness. An anonymous survey would show how content they are with being unmarried, how confident they are of their marriage prospects and whether they feel valued as single people within the church community. You may not have seen as many fall away as I have over relationships and immorality, but I wish the debate could be engaged with hard facts rather than trading anecdotes.

3
The Celibacy Club

Non-Christians say that we are sexually repressed. And they're right. While the *Daily Mirror* reports that the average person has sex 117 times a year, the average single Christian aims at having sex zero times a year. The difference – about 117 times by my arithmetic – means that secular singles see Britain's churches as being full of single Christians depressed about not having sex and feeling emotionally isolated. On the other side of the aisle they see singles who *are* having sex, and who are often racked with guilt about their hypocrisy. Our message to single non-Christians of 'Join our Celibacy Club' is simply not an attractive advertising slogan. Especially when not everyone is playing by the rules.

The culture shock of joining an organisation where sex is off limits to all but the married is enormous. But the growing realisation that a 'legit' sexual partner may not exactly be easy to find is another matter. 'No sex before marriage' may be a novel concept, but 'no sex before death' is no laughing matter. People will not stay.

There are however many non-Christians who find the church's positive message of being faithful to one sexual partner highly attractive. They, both men and women, have been hurt by the world's 'use-and-dispose' sexual attitudes. They want to escape, but fear that becoming a Christian would be a case of jumping out of the frying pan into the freezer.

> **'No sex before marriage' may be a novel concept, but 'no sex before death' is no laughing matter.**

They also find the thinking of the Christian sub-culture at odds with the reality they have lived. Many non-Christians cannot relate to the pastor who says, 'Sex is fun, but only in marriage.' Many found that, at least for a while, sleeping around was fun. Many have been part of relatively strong unmarried relationships. They agree that sexual anarchy destroys relationships, but they themselves have been conducting friendships with a considerable measure of responsibility. There has been much worthwhile about their relationships and they cannot accept the black-and-white castigation of the sexual practices of the secular world.

We also need to purge ourselves of judgemental attitudes in those cases where non-Christians have demonstrably reaped the consequences of sexually wild lives. Not just because 'there but for the grace of God go I', but also because many strong Christians in our congregation were once 'there'! Our message must not come across as, 'You are immoral and we are virtuous.' No, our simple claim is that on the 'product' called relationships we have a copy of the Manufacturer's instructions. By following these instructions and 'phoning the heavenly hotline' for help on specific problems, we argue that everyone will get more satisfaction from the product. The Bible and the help-desk of prayer are both part of the eternal warranty that comes with the product.

To continue the metaphor, whenever I go round a showroom I like the gleamy new look of the products, but I find the sales patter a lot more convincing if I can see the product working. Likewise the church. Many non-Christians are impressed with an initial look at the product and would be happy to trade in their version of relationships. They may even be enthusiastic enough to sign up straightaway by 'saying the prayer'. But then they look beyond our claim that marital faithfulness means that Christians make better lovers. They see the reality of love-starved single Christians struggling in isolated celibacy, and they come across ill-matched Christian couples contemplating divorce.

Perhaps against that backdrop we can better understand the revolving-door tendency where some non-Christians leave church soon after arriving. While there is a host of reasons why they do not remain, many are put off by the way so many Christian singles are perplexed and discontent over being single. They did not find the loving community which Jesus said would be the way the world would know that we are his disciples. They are not persuaded to get to know their Maker and how much he cares for them if they do not see it being lived out among believers.

It is the quality of the role models in our congregation that communicates better than any preacher. Secular singles entering our churches do notice whether or not single Christian men and women are getting to know each other easily. If they also see a number of engaged couples moving steadily towards marriage they will be further impressed. And what completes the picture is the role model of real families which are not just surviving but thriving.

Where non-Christians can see this path being traced out by believers, they will be able mentally to picture themselves walking down the same route if they remain in the church community. Most new converts would be happy to think that they might find a marriage partner in their church, but instead they find single Christians talking about their despair in not finding a partner. To some extent this must add to any disillusionment they feel about their new Christian life.

To be blunt, if a single woman in her late thirties thinks getting married and having children is important, does becoming a Christian make sense? The prospect of no sex, no non-Christian boyfriends, no available Christian men and nobody else dating presents a pretty lousy prospect. Often coming straight out of unmarried relationships, they face extreme pressures to slip back into the world if they suspect that there is little prospect of resuming the comforts of marriage in a 'legitimate' relationship. The failure of many congregations to offer such hope shrinks the church. Great preaching can lead many to faith, but it is only a great church community that will retain them.

While we are on the subject of growing the church, here is an unfashionable thought. There is no better place for evangelism than the home; no more accessible people group to explain the gospel to than our own children. So in churches where single people are not getting married, there are not going to be children who can be raised as Christians. More Christian marriages means more in the church crèche, the toddlers' group, the confirmation class. . . .

'Come, see a man who told me everything I ever did.' This is what the Samaritan woman told her friends after encountering Jesus. Having got through five husbands and currently engaged in cohabitation she is a prototype for our age. Yet, as with the woman caught in adultery, Jesus not only associates with her, but speaks plainly to her.

Like Christ we need to be simultaneously plain-speaking and compassionate in dealing with the relationship problems of those at the edge of faith; to be fully engaged in a sexually muddied world without becoming muddied ourselves. To be 'sheep among wolves' Jesus said we need to be 'wise as snakes and innocent as doves'. Yet in matters of sexuality the church tends to be all dove. We are not wise enough to realise that the main reason some non-Christians (and dare I suggest Christians as well?) come to church is for the opportunity to meet someone. Even where it is not the dominant motivation it can be a powerful secondary one. If our ambition is to win unbelievers to Christ let us acknowledge this, and let us be crafty and wily enough to use this. Arguments are better won if you start by showing understanding of where the other party is at, so sermons addressing non-Christians' earthly concerns about relationships may be a better start than directly trying to get them to catch hold of a heavenly vision. Secular singles may not realise that they need a new spiritual heart, but they do have emotional hearts which are aching.

There are religious cults which manipulate sexual attractiveness in an attempt to win converts. Men and women are lured to meetings under the deception that their 'street evangelist' has some romantic or sexual interest in them. Such 'flirty fishing' is contemptible, but just because male–female attraction is abused and manipulated by some does not mean that we should not be pastorally aware of its real impact on church attendance. We need to be awake to the reality that a key attraction of the church community is that it provides a place where marriages can take place and grow. If this aspect of community life is dysfunctional, it takes away from the attractiveness of church life.

Letter to a church leader

Dear Pastor,

Does your study resemble a hospital accident and emergency ward? Full of pain and tears as you try to patch up the casualties of human folly. Not broken legs, but broken hearts; not diseased bodies, but despairing souls. You move from dealing with the teenage boy who has just been chucked by his first girlfriend, to the single-parent mum who is tempted to sleep with her new boyfriend. Then to the wife who has been deserted by her non-Christian husband, followed by the married couple struggling with their basic lack of compatibility. Tomorrow it will be more of the same.

This constant crisis counselling saps the morale of the most energetic and able minister. Yet amid the phone calls do you have time to reflect on how this tyranny of the desperate is getting in the way of bringing the rest of the congregation to maturity in their faith, of focusing on evangelism, of improving the worship in your church? The common theme behind so much of their hurt and angst is the difficulty of finding and developing relationships with suitable Christians. But is our response as a church misdirected? Instead of concentrating on the pastoral debris of failing relationships, should we be emphasising the preventive – seeking a vision from God on how he would have friendships of all kinds being formed in churches, some of which could provide the foundations of solid marriages?

This is such an important issue, for if the church is to flourish we need to have clear teaching on how God intends men and women to meet, as well as much more prayer on what is an overlooked spiritual battleground. How much systematic prayer goes into the creation of Christian marriages? Is it that much of a surprise then that so many Christians make a bad job of it? If we were to get hold of God's heart on the issue we would not have any embarrassment making it a regular subject for prayer in the church, nor would we worry about the reaction if we organised regular prayer meetings devoted to relationship formation. Many Christians pray a great deal about the issue on their own (often for themselves), so there is a willingness.

When you wrestle with the subject in prayer then maybe God will show you why this issue has not been as high on your agenda as I suspect it is on his. Am I being very malicious to wonder whether a few unmarried church leaders are blinded to the problems of their congregation by the aphrodisiac power of being a 'Christian authority figure'! After all, unmarried curates are often deluged with interest from the opposite sex, and it can be hard to see the problems of those suffering from lack of interest when your main concern is excess attention! And if you are married already, then even if it was ever a struggle finding the right partner, it is now at most a receding memory.

And how much has your theology of relationship formation been governed by your own experience? With hindsight it is easy to ascribe your spouse's arrival as being solely down to the sovereignty of God, yet this sovereign God appears to be deliberately denying the provision of partners to increasing swathes of the church. Maybe I am being too strong. But the hyper-Calvinist view that the process is all down to God and not human initiative does absolve the church from responsibility for addressing the issue.

There is a balance that needs to be struck between encouraging people to rest in the assurance of God's sovereign provision and helping them to help themselves. You don't have to swallow the Arminian angle of 'choose whoever you want so long as they're a Christian' to think that some action would be helpful. Perhaps there is a role for churches either on their own or with others to hold monthly meetings for their singles in their twenties and thirties. Some churches do this already. They see that if they do not provide such a meeting place for their unmarrieds then at best their singles will use church services to 'size up the talent' and at worst they will give up hope and start dating non-Christians. Maybe there is also a role for church leaders to suggest matches between their congregations. Such matchmaking was once common practice in the church. The only reason it hasn't been so for a long time is that it runs counter to our individualistic culture.

One thing we most definitely need is to hear the word of God clearly from the pulpit – messages of God's blessing on singleness as well as on marriage, and of his prohibition of sex outside marriage. It is frightening how many Christians are unaware of the basics because they are not preached. Sure, teaching against immorality from the pulpit will stir up a hornets' nest, but just as Paul showed the backbone to repeatedly and publically denounce sexual immorality in the church, so must you. Singles are crying out for clear, direct guidance.

By speaking God's word into relationships we are speaking life into a nation of dying relationships. The more friendships that are formed, the more Christian community deepens and the church once again becomes the radical counter-culture of the Book of Acts. The world recognises that it is failing in relationships and it expects the situation to get even worse. Amid the deepening gloom a church where real community exists – and that is impossible without relationship formation – will shine all the more brightly.

Yours

Ian Gregory

SECTION TWO
Why We Are Still Single

4
Hiding from Commitment

I am scared of marriage – scared that having made myself vulnerable to love, she might walk out. Years of devotion, of becoming one through thick and thin ended in a note on the kitchen table saying, 'I'm not coming back.' I'm scared that because of bitterness or selfishness she will use all her feminine wiles to make it difficult for me to see my children. I'm fearful that having robbed me of the people I love she will then remove me from my home, pursue me endlessly through the courts for maintenance . . . and set the Child Support Agency on me. I'm fearful of lying on my empty bed, thinking of how my friends are discussing how much I was to blame, and that while I am alone again, she is with him.

And you, sister, are also scared – scared that he will walk out on you when you are five months pregnant; after you have given up your full-time career, and your figure has begun to go. You are scared that the world of glittering prizes that you gave up for him will be swapped for days of filling in social security forms. You are scared that the children will blame you for Daddy's going, and that

while you are in your emotional bereftness they will
need you to be Father, Mother and provider. You
think of the stares and knowing looks at church,
and you think, 'What other man would want me
how I am?'

No idle fears these. For as a child you witnessed it
all. The screaming, the tears, the slamming doors.
How could you put yourself through that, let alone
your children? Even if your mind is not afraid, then
from deep within your emotions cry out for caution.

If not divorce then death may have torn our parents (and with them us) apart. A subconscious
warning light in our souls warns us against making
ourselves emotionally dependent on mere flesh and
blood. Where our parents' marriage did survive the
twin traumas of premature death and divorce (and
less than half of marriages reach twenty-five years),
then it may still not have been a good advertisement
for commitment.

**Some of us seek refuge in relation-
ships that inwardly we know will not
work in order to avoid confronting
our own unwillingness to take the
risk of marriage.**

To add to our parents' experience comes our own
– of being dropped, of broken engagements or of
separating from a cohabiting partner. The older we
are, the more wounds we have and the more we are
once bitten twice shy. We are like Pavlov's dogs: the

words 'relationship' and 'marriage' trigger thoughts of pain in our mind.

The result is that many of us have got to the stage where we are for ever running away. Running away from men and women we love being with because the desire to be with them is overwhelmed by the fear of losing them. Some of us seek refuge in relationships that inwardly we know will not work in order to avoid confronting our own unwillingness to take the risk of marriage.

Marrying a Christian is no guarantee against divorce, but this is no reason not to marry. Take the analogy of driving a car. There is no certainty each time I get into my car that I will not be involved in a bad crash, yet since I am determined not to stay isolated in my home I do drive. However, I do take precautions: wearing my seatbelt, not driving too fast, keeping the car well maintained. I may still have a bad smash, but the risks are that much less. The emotional carnage of a divorce is always possible in that our partners have been given free will by God and thus have the ability to walk out on us at any stage. Even if you are the most loving and wise spouse there is still no guarantee – just a much lower likelihood of having to crawl out of the wreckage of a smashed relationship. So let us confront our fears, not be imprisoned by them. Faith is about taking risks for God. Wisdom is heavenly commonsense about how we take those risks. Remaining single out of fear is not compatible with a healthy walk with God. Whatever our hurts, whatever our fears, we need to surrender them to God if we are to be free to make choices.

It is not difficult to see what feeds our fears. So much of our nation's emotional landscape is littered with wrecked lives – from the Royal Family to our next door neighbour – that to raise our faith in marriage we must consciously search out good role models to focus on. Spending time with married couples whose relationships are thriving gives us faith and vision about what we too could enjoy.

Unless we are meeting lots of 'real' married couples in our communities an equal but opposite issue can lead us to run away from relationships: the illusion that marriage partners must have no defects. We meet someone and discover some flaw and we're not interested, but since we all have flaws, we are in reality hiding from marriage. Singles attending predominantly singles churches tend to develop an 'alabaster' vision of marriage in which two perfectly matched human beings spend their time in a bliss world of no arguments, disagreements or rows. We miss out on the truth that marriages grow because there are differences that are being worked out, not because they are absent. In my work it is the tackling and solving of acute problems that makes me grow as a television producer – not the (rare) days when everything goes smoothly.

Neither the 'marriages are destined to fail' thought pattern nor the 'alabaster' vision of perfection will encourage us to find a well-matched partner. But there are two other ways that society has patterned our minds which are even worse in making us 'marriage-shy'. 'Me first' individualism and the desire for instant relationships cripple us from finding and forming relationships.

When earlier this century would-be immigrants to America arrived in New York they would be given a 'six-second medical'. As they walked up the stairs to the immigration hall of Ellis Island, medical inspectors would watch them and then chalk on them an 'R' for respiratory problems, an 'L' for lameness or an 'X' for appearing feeble-minded – an instant judgement that would determine the direction of a person's life. Now isn't that often the way we assess members of the opposite sex?

'That'll be a McMarriagePartner with good looks and extra high income' is our fast-food approach to dating. We know what we want, we want it now and nothing less will satisfy. Growing into love? No way! If you don't make me tingle in all the right places right now then we're not even going to get to the first date. No sense in getting to know your personality or your character – the parts of you that have taken decades to develop and would hold the marriage together for the decades to come. Sorry, as you walked up the stairs to church you didn't pass the 'Ian Gregory score card for potential partners' based on a weighted average of age, IQ, looks and emotional stability. We need to tear up our graphs and spend time getting to know the whole person before we make judgements. It's called dating.

After our instant assessment of each other, we want instant depth. Before our sapling friendship has a chance to grow we are weighing it down with emotional and physical demands which it is incapable of carrying. But the biggest risk to that sapling is that the soil of romance is poisoned by individualism. It is hard to underestimate the way individualism has seeped into all our thinking processes. Individual freedom is the unofficial religion of the 1990s. Absolutely nothing is more important than my current assessment of what will make me happy. I am free to abandon any commitment if it gets in the way of that goal. Being a husband, a father, an employer or an employee – nothing is sacrosanct. The only thing that binds any two human beings together is that for the moment they find it mutually advantageous.

Even the language of commitment seems archaic. 'Loyalty, honour, vows, promises, trust, troth and fidelity are words from a dying tongue. Few in our generation understand the idea of covenant, so the concept of marriage as covenant has eluded us; that you and I take each other on, to love each other through our failings as much as through our successes: 'For better, for worse, for richer, for poorer, in sickness and in health as long as we both shall live.' It is this commitment to stay with each other and be there for each other during the down times that is the unique and amazing formula of marriage.

The marriage covenant is God's antidote to the twentieth century. Will you stay with me when my employer has sacked me to boost next month's profits? When our home is being compulsorily purchased to make way for road widening? When our children are being rebels? When some fat cat financier has stolen our pension? When I'm dying of multiple sclerosis? Will you be with me when all your friends say that it is not in your interests to stay?

Society teaches us that we should run away from such commitment, such covenant love. Our generation has been taught to treat marriage as a conditional contract in which the central clause is 'as long as we both shall be happy'. To our neighbours it is not only acceptable to walk out, but ridiculous not to do so if you are unhappy. But the church teaches us that it should be 'as long as we both shall live'. So we are torn between the world and the church, between contract and covenant. While we would love the certainty of covenant, we do not know whether we or our potential partners have the desire and the ability to cut free from the world's view.

> **Marriage is under stress because it runs so totally opposed to the values of our age. And that is precisely why marriage is so remarkably valuable.**

Let us encourage ourselves that only covenant marriage is truly satisfying. It draws strength from our past together as well as our future, whereas contract marriage is only based on a series of conditional 'nows'. Let us start learning the process of commitment and honour with the people around us – our friends, our colleagues, the people we date. If we can throw off the shackles of individualism in these shorter-term relationships, then not only will we live better lives this year, but we will also be better prepared for the immense challenge of marriage.

Individualism is not only the enemy of covenant. It is also behind the modern creed of 'keeping your options open'. With relationships this leads us perpetually to delay marriage. We can never rule out that there might be someone better round the corner, so we for ever put off the decision to marry. It may seem as though we are preserving our options and our freedom, but we wake up in our thirties to realise that we will never have the option of being married in our twenties; never have the option of marrying the man or woman we turned down some years ago and who has now married someone else; and probably never have the chance of celebrating a golden wedding anniversary.

Our fierce commitment to our freedom leaves us as islands. That is very little, because our lives are composed of the choices we make, not the choices we avoid. Our lives are the sum of the people we relate to – at home, at work, socially – not the people we don't relate to. So if we become the ideal of individualism that our society aspires to – utterly free from all binding commitments – then we have become utterly nothing. To endlessly avoid making binding commitments denies that in making those very pledges, we are expressing our freedom. In limiting ourselves to one person we are decisively showing our generation that we Christians are the free ones. We have chosen the freedom that they are scared of – the freedom of limiting ourselves to one person for life. And if our identity is securely wrapped up in Christ, then even if our partner should die or desert us we will still not be alone.

Individualism masquerades under many guises. The consumerism that tells us that if it doesn't work we can change it should not be brought into marriage. Neither should women bring in the more self-centred aspects of feminism. That said, all Christian husbands should be feminists, so that in obeying Paul's injunction to love their wives as their own bodies, they actively look for ways of encouraging their wives' intellectual and creative gifts. They need to share enough of the burden of child-caring and home-making to ensure that their wives have the opportunity to grow as persons outside the home. But if wives bring the 'me' of feminism into relationships the effect is to stunt the growth of oneness. In the same way that a generation ago men broke up marriages by their insistence on putting their jobs first, some women now avoid marriage by putting their careers first.

Careerism is a final form of individualism that leads us to avoid marriage. So many singles consider their job to be their number one priority, and they become too busy to date properly and even psychologically incapable of putting a member of the opposite sex before their work. We cannot have two things as our number one priority. So which is it to be? And don't say, 'Job now, marriage later.' Your work habits will pursue you into marriage. As single Christians rise up their career structures, they become more dominated by the work place and less capable of developing intimacy. Men and women who are consciously or subconsciously delaying marriage for the sake of their careers need to think ahead to when they retire. Forced to choose, I would be much happier to reflect on 'my brilliant marriage' than on 'my brilliant career'.

Welcome to the KYOO Retirement Home!

I have a dream (or is it a nightmare?) of a whole gang of us meeting up at some retirement home. In it I see that while we are a bit doddery now, we are still reasonably alert. And all of us are still single. Yet we don't seem to be at all worried about delaying marriage so late. Instead we're congratulating each other on how we've managed to stay single for so long. Residents of the Keep Your Options Open Retirement Home all know that Mr or Miss Right may join the home at any time. So it's worth waiting. None of us is willing to settle for second best. As we prowl around the corridors with our zimmer frames, eyeing up the talent, we're as fussy as ever.

Just occasionally, following their afternoon nap, one of the residents will wonder out loud what would have happened if they had gone ahead and married one of their loves a few decades earlier. But the rest of us just chorus, 'You had a narrow escape, old bean!' Every now and then one of us fails to wake up from our nap. In truth we are all a bit jealous of them. After all, they'll never have to fret about putting off decisions again.

5
I Don't Have a Problem with Denial

Denial is a difficult subject to deal with, for it involves diving deep into the submerged parts of our subconscious to examine thought processes that we have kept hidden not only from others, but also from ourselves. If spotting self-deception in our friends is tricky, it is much, much harder to see it at work in our own minds. What we can be sure of is that for all of us, the layers of events that we have experienced through life have created in us our own unique psychological make-up.

A very controlling parent, a traumatic bereavement or a history of sexual abuse – experiences like these, especially if they came early in our lives, can badly scar our subconscious in ways that we do not fully recognise. Even though you and I may be unaware of our subconscious being at work, it can still be provoking strong responses in us – not least in our reaction to the opposite sex. It is hard for me to assess whether splitting up with the woman I was engaged to four years ago still has an impact on me. Certainly time has healed, but I can still vividly recall the two of us quaking with tears as we separated.

Our hidden inner fears of being hurt again may lead us to a reluctance to enter or stay in long-term relationships. It is often glibly labelled 'commitment-phobia', but there is nothing straightforward about a subject which has a habit of torpedoing every romance that sails into our life.

The symptoms of romantic denial are numerous. They are seen in the way we chase people who, if truth be told, are deeply unsuitable for us while simultaneously fending off highly eligible members of the opposite sex. Romantic denial is about the way we effectively ensure our isolation by pursuing members of the opposite sex with whom there is no realistic hope of achieving a lasting relationship. For instance, where they live on the other side of the world . . . literally.

Next month a plane from Sydney will land at Heathrow Airport carrying a very attractive Australian woman. She is coming to see a male friend of mine who met her in Australia last year. They were so strongly attracted to each other during that first meeting that she is spending a day on a jumbo jet to be able to see him. How very sweet . . . or how very daft?

Let us get this clear. There is nothing intrinsically wrong with transoceanic relationships based on deep commitment. If these two Christians get on well with each other and eventually marry then I will be thrilled. My whole purpose in writing this book is to encourage lasting relationships. But is this woman's trip a voyage to commitment or a flight of fancy? For by all accounts this Australian should not be short of potential suitors at home. Now I'm not denying that my friend is a decent 'catch' (I daren't because he will be reading this!), but amid his understandable feelings of flattery that this woman is traversing the planet for a second date with him, let us wonder whether he or she has stopped to think whether they are pursuing romance or relationship. Living on opposite sides of the world, the chance of their friendship being able to grow to the point where they are ready to make a decision to marry is remote. Instead, the romantic fantasy which is impoverishing her financially, as well as preoccupying her thoughts, may be serving another purpose: helping her to avoid facing up to the reality of the men she could form committed relationships with in Australia, and facing up to her real life in Sydney instead of her fantasy life in London. This woman thinks that she is taking finding a partner seriously – for goodness sake she *is* flying to England! But the degree of energy involved may merely be blinding her to her inner uncertainty about relationships. The key question is this: Are these two using their romance as a means of avoiding a commitment or as a route to making one?

And what about you and me? When you look back at your romantic past and ask yourself about the deeper reasons why your relationships ended – indeed, why you got involved in them in the first place – do you see any patterns? Serial dating of no-hopers? Fixations on the best-looking person in your church? Chasing people who while not needing a passport to visit are not going to be easy to get to know? Or ending relationships when they were becoming close? Such patterns – and there are many more variations on the theme – betray that we are operating on two levels. On the surface our words and actions show a desire to find a partner. But at a subconscious level we are being motivated by fears that are diverting our romantic energy down paths that have little hope of creating lasting relationships.

When you look back at your romantic past and ask yourself about the deeper reasons why your relationships ended – indeed, why you got involved in them in the first place – do you see any patterns?

The fears that drive us and the ways they sabotage our romantic lives differ between the sexes. Let's deal with simple things first. Men.

The male is traditionally seen as the more 'commitmentphobic' of the species. Let's face it, we're raised to believe that we're biologically programmed to sow wild oats while avoiding being tied down into a relationship. It is a way of life that has been given a great boost by the sexual 'liberation' of the 1960s, which has meant that men feel they can expect to get into the bedroom without being required to give any commitment in return. In short, we marriage-avoiding men are supposed to have a good time and keep our options open.

Hollywood has reinforced the image with films which show women relentlessly seeking out a man who takes a great deal of convincing before entering a relationship: *Pretty Woman*, *Sleepless in Seattle* and *Casablanca*. All have a woman obsessed with a man who is shy of getting serious. It's not just American culture to blame. At school I remember our class being taught the ancient song in which a maid repeatedly sings the line, 'Soldier, Soldier, will you marry me with your musket, fife and drum?' to which the soldier comes up with a series of lame excuses until he finally confesses that he cannot marry her 'Because I have a wife of my own'! So the unreliable commitmentphobic man is a long-standing cultural stereotype.

If that is how we men have been told we behave, then it is no big surprise when we start thinking, at least subconsciously, that this is the way we should behave. But there are other subtler reasons why men get into relationships that are doomed from the start. For instance, we may get involved with a much younger woman because we are afraid of getting old. Or because she, being at the start of her career, is untarnished by failure, thus making an attractive escape for the older man who is haunted by the lack of progress in his own working life.

The growing economic independence of women can further add to a man's fear of committing his life to a real relationship. For there dawns on a man the realisation that the woman he is thinking of marrying has the financial means to walk away if

she feels that it isn't working out. It could be a
fear that his father didn't have to face up to because
his wife didn't have a strong career at her disposal.
   Now to more complex matters.

> Women are in fact unacknowledged masters of
> ambivalence – giving passionate lip service to their
> desire for relationships while secretly avoiding, even
> sabotaging, potential involvements ... we have
> become adept at keeping secrets from ourselves, even
> about something as apparently straightforward as our
> romantic availability. (Sheila Gillooly, *Venus in Spurs*
> [Hodder & Stoughton, 1996])

The assumption that men are the commitmentphobics, that they're the jilting gender, has served
as a smokescreen stopping women from detecting
their own inner uncertainties over relationships.
Those submerged fears have increased over the past
few decades as a result of the radical changes in
women's role in society. A generation ago we were
still very much a male-dominated society. And in
patriarchies where power is in male hands, it is
imperative for a woman to be linked with a man in
marriage. Now before anyone objects, I agree that
there are still many bastions of male domination that
have yet to fall. But the changes that have occurred
are nothing short of revolutionary. So while your
mother may assume that marriage is still a must,
you perceive it to be a choice. A single life is now
much more acceptable with your peer group in terms
of status. Often it is the biological desire to have
children that swings the decision towards marriage.

This debate – to marry or not to marry – may have been settled on the surface, but it may still be raging in a woman's subconscious mind. And it is this hidden debate that is revealed in a whole range of self-defeating romantic behaviour that Sheila Gillooly and other writers are beginning to identify. Take, for a start, having romances with men you strongly suspect are gay. Now there are lots of positive reasons for doing this. First, they are often physically attractive, sensitive men who are more than capable of talking about emotions. Also, they are not sexually pushy – at least not with women! But the greatest attraction to dating them, as far as a commitment-phobic woman is concerned, is that such a relationship can both satisfy the romantic impulse and yet not set off the inner warning bells about commitment.

The same type of arguments apply to dating married men, or pursuing men who are in reality unavailable. Take, for example, the music leader at a big English church. After his engagement was announced, seventeen women went for counselling. They had been living in the fantasy that he was meant for them. Going from the sublime to the ridiculous, what about dating dunderheads or exotic, 'dangerous' men? Men with whom a long-term relationship is not going to work?

Consider a friend of mine called Helen. Now in her thirties, the five serious loves of her life fall into two categories: men who have just been dumped by their fiancées (three of them) or men who are philanderers (the other two). Helen explains the former

as being her living out her role as a 'heart mender' —
her father died when she was eight, so she spent a lot
of her childhood comforting her mother. So for these
men who had lost their girlfriends she offered comfort until they, having been healed of their hurt, got
up and left, embarrassed at having shown their
weakness. As for the philanderers, Helen feels that
she did well when these guys — used to one night
stands — stayed with her for six months. Like with
her three heartbroken boyfriends, she 'knew they
would not stay', so she was spared the trauma of
having a repeat of the disaster that happened when
she was eight — the man at the centre of her life
dying.

All such relationships allow the fantasy of
romance to be conducted while shielding you from
deepening relationships and ultimately yourself as
well. For this is the heart of the matter. In genuine
intimacy someone is getting to see the real you. They
act as a mirror in which you see yourself as you are.
And since romantic fantasy has given way to rela-
tional reality you no longer have anything distracting
you from the day-to-day truths of your life. Often we
find it much easier to remain in unreality.

I hate to give any ammunition to patronising married couples who look on singles as incomplete, but
it is true that committed long-term relationships can
be a very maturing process. For it is in the close
interaction of people that we are being extended
and challenged. Such vulnerability to another person
and through them to themselves is the stuff of night-
mares for us commitmentphobics. So we put up the

shutters on eligible members of the opposite sex. And if one should accidentally arrive in our life, then we marriage-avoiders will subconsciously be looking for ways out of the relationship.

Perhaps you are a 'Desperate Dalek' who relentlessly pursues relationships with robotic determination and then equally clinically finds yourself in 'destroy, destroy' mode when things get too close? Or are you a 'Perpetual Postponer', holding off from relationships until the biological clock starts to chime midnight?

I think I can picture your nightmare vision of the future: you, the aspiring concert pianist, being taken by your husband's career as a missionary to some remote part of Africa where the nearest piano is four days' trek and hasn't been tuned since the war. Instead, babies arrive and your fingers begin handwringing a never ending stream of cotton nappies as your husband seeks to convert the natives in some distant village.

Other forms of female commitmentphobia include regarding all men as sex fiends or being obsessive about keeping all relationships under control. As soon as they get out of control – that is, you start getting fond of him – then it's time to call it a day. Food is another weapon for the commitment-averse. What better way to get him to leave than to start overeating in order to become a bloated version of the woman he was first attracted to?

Janet, who lives in California, suspected that her boyfriend, Tom, was cheating on her. She didn't feel confident enough to confront him or drop him. She says: 'I was miserable in the relationship, but I feared that I might never meet anyone else. So I got fat to force him to break up with me. He also liked my long hair, which went right down my back, so I cut it really short!'

Janet is probably well rid of Tom, but our subconscious can equally wreck good relationships or propel us into strong commitments to deeply unattractive people. For example, the children of alcoholics, batterers or abusers are more likely to marry partners with exactly the same problem. Perversely, the very people who have suffered from being raised in such families, having developed the emotional habits for supporting their failing parent, find it hard to turn away potential partners with identical failings because it enables them to continue in that supporting role. This attraction to the familiar is reinforced by the low self-esteem that characterises the children of dysfunctional homes, along with an inability to recognise appropriate behaviour. If violence has been part of domestic life from your earliest memories, it is hard to see what appropriate boundaries of behaviour are. And without this innate sense of the appropriate we are going to find it harder to attract 'normal' partners. This patterning can run so deep that the daughter of an alcoholic father who has married an alcoholic man can find it difficult to adjust if he is cured.

If some of these examples strike a chord in your own life, then what can you do to avoid wasting even more of your life chasing or living in nonrelationships? The key is understanding that our focus must be on ourselves first – sorting out our thinking to decide which of our fears should be dispensed with. Only when the war within is settled can we peacefully decide to stay single or enter and remain in a stable relationship. Sometimes such thinking is only undertaken in the aftermath of yet another failed romance. Sometimes the best way to confront your fears is by taking the leap of faith and stepping into a relationship with someone suitable, patiently working through your fears together.

Much of this chapter has focused on women's romantic denial. That is simply because it is still less well recognised than male commitmentphobia. But both genders need to stop habitually blaming the opposite sex for the failure of their relationships. Instead we need to know ourselves and our fears well enough to see how they have been propelling us into and out of relationships. Only when, through prayer and counsel, we have let Jesus release us from these fears will we be free to choose the type of relationship we really want.

6
Confidence – the Lubricant of Life

If the love of your life dumps you it may not have been commitmentphobia they were suffering from. Perhaps it was claustrophobia! Were you holding on to them just a little too tightly? For excessive eagerness to commit can be just as fatal as a desire to avoid commitment. Any lack of self-confidence in a relationship can result in the flame of romance being smothered. So are you secretly afraid that no one suitable would want to commit to you?

Such lack of confidence comes in different forms. Our surface thoughts may tell us: 'I'm too ugly, too old, too stupid and too poor for anyone to want to marry me.' Deeper down there are more gnawing fears that make us feel that the world is a hostile place and that we had better batten down the hatches to stop nasty things happening to us. These fears, often stemming from words and events that traumatised us when we were young, may have been reinforced by struggles in our lives as single adults. Take, for example, my day-by-day battle to find work during the recession of the early 1990s. It left me with a battered self-confidence that expected rejection not acceptance. Such a lack of confidence is a disease that devastates our romantic chances. At a basic level we realise that if we do not like and respect ourselves then we can't really expect anyone else to. If our vocabulary is full of self-deprecation, and our body language displays insecurity, then the opposite sex will not be interested in us. People have enough problems of their own, without seeking to add another set! Fundamentally we understand that a person who does not love themselves is unable to love others. My future wife will not be able to love me more than she loves herself. So I'd better look after her! Does this reasoning lie behind Paul arguing that husbands should love their wives 'as their own bodies' and Jesus saying, 'Love your neighbour as yourself'?

It is because we know that people who lack confidence make lousy lovers that we are so keen to hide our lack of confidence. If there's one thing that we are more afraid of than being left on the shelf, it is being seen to be desperate! When we lack confidence we regard dating as an opportunity for being rejected rather than an opportunity to meet someone who will love us. In this game of romance, so much can depend on a fleeting moment – catching his eye, seizing the chance to ask for her phone number – that any paralysis by fear fatally undermines our chances. We are frozen from taking the necessary risks because we are petrified of being rejected.

It's 'Catch-22'. When I get married I will feel more confident, but how do I find someone worth marrying when I am so short of confidence? Around us we see confident people winning over those we would like to be with. Some of them are a lot less good-looking than we are! Who will rid me of this lack of self-confidence?

I have three suggestions. The first is that there is an amazing amount that we can do ourselves to boost our self-respect. If we start to take charge of our lives in our day-to-day choices instead of seeing ourselves as victims of life, our confidence will rise and things we never dreamed of will come into reach. It becomes a virtuous spiral as rising confidence prompts us to take more steps which further boost our confidence. Look at your life and see what is knocking your confidence and try to change these areas. If you lack education, go on a course. If your boss is constantly criticising you, change jobs. If a relationship you are in is undermining your faith, get out of it. For me a watershed was moving home. I was deeply unhappy where I was, but to move away meant losing the little security I had. Like so many of the key decisions in life, it was very hard at first, but has subsequently proved so worthwhile.

The second suggestion is to get help. Often our friends and pastors aren't able to provide the encouragement or wisdom that we require, and we need to get outside help. I would much prefer a Christian therapist to a secular one, but you must shop around until you find someone with the skills and the time to help you understand yourself. While Americans think nothing of going to their therapist, British reserve combines with our belief that therapy is only for the mentally ill to stop us getting help. It is hardly surprising that we are such a troubled nation. So get help – unless you enjoy being unhappy. And for the record, unhappy people are always unattractive, however good-looking they are.

There is nothing more liberating than good theology.

Thirdly, there is nothing more liberating than good theology, so get stuck into your Bible to hear God's message for you. 'The Holy Spirit can . . . ultimately heal us from the years of pain,' writes Elaine Storkey in *The Search for Intimacy.* She continues: 'All those damages and hurts which lie deep within our memories and prevent us from knowing freedom in our lives can die themselves as they are swallowed up in the greater love which speaks peace to the depths of our souls.'

There is so much great emotional medicine in Scripture! And we need to pray to the Healer of our souls. I love the tale of the Christian man who put a picture of a gorgeous woman up in his room, under which were the words: 'Your heavenly Father knows you need these things.' Then there was the Christian woman who draped a pair of men's trousers over her bed and prayed every night for God to find a man to fill them – until he did!

As well as praying for provision we need to pray daily for the ability to forgive where we are bitter, for forgiveness is a divine command not so much for the benefit of those who have hurt us – whether it was parents, siblings, neighbours or lovers – but for our own good, so that we can start again. By forgiving those who have hurt us we also become free to move into new relationships. It is no use trying to start the new when we are loaded down with baggage from the old. Bitterness is too heavy a load to carry on our backs.

Here is another liberating paradox from the New Testament. It is only when in our hearts we are free to be single that we are completely free to be married. If in any sense we feel compelled to get married, then we are not making an entirely free choice when we marry.

Take sexual pressure. While the world believes that our sexual drive has to be expressed and that we are of unsound mind if we 'repress' it, the Christian faith declares that our sexuality is something that can and should be disciplined. We do not have to surrender to our impulses, and by living full and vigorous lives despite our 'lack' of sexual intercourse, we power-fully demonstrate to the world that sex is not a god.

Similarly the pressure to have children drives many into ill-suited and often ill-fated marriages. But the New Testament declares that in the church we already have a family. We do not have to have our own genetic children when we fully comprehend the God-given family we have been born into. Rather we see that we have already been given a responsibility to assist parents in the church in sharing the burden and pleasures of raising children. For they are chil-dren of the church as much as of their biological parents. Nor do I have to have my own sons to ensure that my surname survives into the future. That is because the resurrection means that I live on in eternity even after my earthly body is gone.

If a sense of being unvalued is propelling us towards marriage, then again we need to breathe in some good theology. In his book *Families at the Crossroads*, Rodney Clapp reminds us that while 'married Christians have the missionary advantage of hospitality . . . the single Christian has the missionary advantage of mobility'. Swapping singleness for marriage simply changes the framework by which we can serve God. Today I can offer God the ability to go any place any time. When married, my wife and I will be able to offer a hub of stability for those around us. The apostle Paul, of course, considered that singleness had the edge!

In fully functioning Christians, being single or married reveals something of the nature of God, as well as drawing them closer to him. For just as marriage reveals the covenant nature of the Trinity, so in our singleness we demonstrate our total reliance on God. And however excellent our earthly relationships are, our souls will never be truly satisfied without a strong relationship with God. As Elaine Storkey puts it: 'Ultimately the search for intimacy is the search for God.'

Gender perplexed

In the beginning God made us male and female. And it is our confusion about what masculinity and femininity are that contributes to our hesitance in romance. Should a man still make all the moves? Should a man 'chase a woman until she catches him'? Or does our modern view of gender make such notions offensive? When all our assumptions are constantly being challenged, it is no surprise that we lack confidence about the proper way to proceed. If Christian man is wary of being seen by Christian woman as a sexual predator, then he will not make a move; being in any way sexually forward means he risks being labelled either morally dubious or politically incorrect. For example, I am torn between laughter and tears when a friend of mine recounts how difficult a particular Christian woman is to woo. He and his current 'interest' are quite well matched and very keen on each other. Sometimes she is the feminist pursuing him passionately, but on other occasions she is the demure Christian denouncing him as 'a danger to women'. He will phone and be told, 'Don't come round this evening. But I will be in later on.'

Such contradictory messages come from contradictory thinking. Instead of directly addressing her fear that she will lose self-control, she is spiritualising it by saying, 'God has told me that we shouldn't be going out.' Bringing God into the equation closes down discussion. After all, she can't disobey God. But I suspect that God is more interested in dealing with the heart of the problem – in this case how the two of them are both responsible for conducting a holy relationship – rather than stopping the relationship in its tracks. Sadly, the more contradictory 'push and pull' messages my friend gets, the more discouraged he will become. They will go their separate ways. And one day they may bitterly regret it.

Between the extreme views that 'men should do all the chasing' and 'both genders should feel free to make a move' there is a wide range of options. It would be so convenient if everybody was at the same point on that continuum, so that we would know what to expect. But since in our fast-changing world everyone has a different stance, we as individuals must work out our own view and stick to it. We need to be very honest with each other and cautious before we criticise those with different approaches.

We need also to be understanding of the gender differences in our emotional training. Men are generally poorly coached by life in the skill of being emotionally articulate. By contrast, women are often aware of the nuances of a non-verbal conversation which men didn't even realise was taking place. Unless we are confident, we will not have the patience to learn each other's language.

Playing hard to get

Playing hard to get is a game beloved by women who want to dress up their lack of confidence in clothes which have a superficial look of assertiveness. By insisting that men must repeatedly demonstrate their emotional commitment, a woman appears to be exercising control. But behind that mask is the unwillingness of a woman to display her own emotions – a fear of rejection.

This syndrome comes in various guises. I recall that after being interrogated by a group of Christian women about 'how men think' (or was it 'do men think?'?), they said that they would automatically turn a man down the first time he asked them out to ensure that he was keen. In New York a popular new book called *The Rules* is entirely based on this 'playing hard to get' theory. This secular dating manual urges women always to end telephone calls and dates early to indicate how busy they are. Readers are advised that men will become keener if the woman they admire feigns disinterest. (In a remarkable insight into modern definitions of self-restraint, the authors recommend refraining from having sex on the first two dates!)

Well, I have news for women who treat men as puppets on a string. Men of insight will see through it. And many of those who don't will either become bored or assume you are genuinely not interested. Either way, they'll walk off. Women need to learn that they can be friendly and communicative with men while holding on to their dignity and self-respect. Avoiding appearing over-eager is one thing. Being manipulative is quite another.

If we want the dating process to work smoothly, we need to combine confidence with clarity. Let your 'yes' be 'yes' and your 'no' be 'no'!

The danger of the 'playing hard to get' routine is that it combines perniciously with male confusion about whether or not men should be doing all the chasing. If we make a move we are either tarred with the brush of being too foward or given a cool reception by a woman desperate not to appear over-eager. Now we start to see why many women complain that nobody asks them out.

If we want the dating process to work smoothly, we need to combine confidence with clarity. Let your 'yes' be 'yes' and your 'no' be 'no'! It is a lack of confidence in her own attractiveness that leads a woman to be opaque even if she is interested. And so a vicious circle develops, with the man who does press through his uncertainty to ask a woman out finding her unresponsive (not realising that this was a tactic of hers not to appear too keen). Having in his mind been turned down he stops pursuing her (or else he fears he will be accused of harassing her). His confidence is knocked and he is less likely to ask other women out. And as for her, the feeling that this man, like the rest, was only superficially interested in her will undermine her self-image. That will make her even more inclined to ensure that men are really keen on her, by playing still harder to get.

So men and women who lack confidence find their dating lives drying up. Others have the self-assurance to break through the opposite sex's fears. These are the men who persist through the 'playing hard to get' tactics and the women who have the confidence to respond enthusiastically when men they like show an interest. To these people belongs the world of romance. So those who have get more, while those who do not have, even the little they have will be taken from them.

Confidence is the lubricant of life. It stops the engine of our social lives seizing up. We must build up our reserves. Sometimes we lack confidence because our early years were difficult, or we've been wounded by the struggles of adult life. Often, far too often, a lack of confidence in dealing with the opposite sex has been down to bad sexual experiences . . . more on that in Chapter 8.

7
When Then?

Having looked at the way our inner fears and uncertainties wreak havoc on our romantic life, this chapter turns to the highly rational reasons why some Christians are deliberately delaying looking for a marriage partner and asks the question: What is the best age to get married?

Well, biologically speaking, fifteen years old has a lot to recommend it! Young fit bodies don't just produce fit offspring, they also have plenty of physical energy left to cope with those endless broken nights that being a parent entails. But apart from being illegal (and what security is there in an illegal union?) the lack of emotional maturity in teenage relationships is invariably disastrous to both the couple and their child. The child of teenage parents is more likely to be battered and more likely to have its mother and father split up than if they had been in their twenties.

So fifteen is absurd. But when exactly are we emotionally ready for marriage and being parents? When, in terms of the balance between biological, emotional and career development, is the ideal time to marry?

Let us go to the other extreme. Many people in our generation are leaving nuptials until they are thirty-five plus. This does have its merits. At that age it is likely that people's careers are well developed and they have sorted themselves out after the woes of their twenties. They are also often much clearer about the type of partner they are after and (assuming their potential spouse is of a similiar age) they can see whether he or she is destined to be one of life's successes or failures.

But dominating the whole debate is the issue of biological clocks. And here, as a man, I try to tread very gingerly. For women need no reminders of the impact of age on fertility and on the health of mother and child. Most women who have passed their early thirties would say that they did not intend to leave it this late. For a host of reasons – some of which were raised in earlier chapters – they have not yet met a man they are happy with being the father of their children. The intense pressure of getting established in a competitive career does not make that search any easier. It is hard to find a husband if you are married to the job. But equally should one throw away hard-won career opportunities simply to hang around for a man?

Men, in response, so easily get into double standards. They see themselves as being wise to delay marriage and women as being foolish – the image of the 'sad old spinster' versus the 'sensible man'. But do men have a point in being miffed by women who give the appearance of having held off committing themselves to a relationship until they have to? The tendency of modern women to leave marriage until later adds to the intense pressures for Christian men in living a pure life in the middle of a sexually immoral society. Our libidos have been awake since our early teens. Not desperately helpful if our potential partners are not in the 'marrying mood' until their thirties. And, while the reality may be different, the perception to a man can be that a woman sees her career as being much more important than marriage and children. Like women, no man wants to play second fiddle to a career. Nor do they want to feel compelled to start a family quickly after marriage – or indeed face a high risk of not having children at all. This male unease about marrying older women is reflected in statistics which show a second and less well-documented problem facing women who make a late dash to the altar: a lousy choice of men. The paper *Availability of marriage partners in England and Wales*, by the sociologist Richard Lampard, has buried within it a fascinating table. Using census data it shows that for every 100 women aged between twenty and twenty-four there are 157 men chasing them. Loads of choice! But ten years later, in the age range thirty to thirty-four, it is down to ninety-one men. For women between the ages of forty and forty-four it is reduced to seventy-eight men. So in the first ten years the choice of men has fallen by 43 per cent. And while twenty years on there are still a reasonable number of men available, it is half the number who were interested. There is also evidence that the average 'quality' of those men left 'on the shelf' is also lower. The reason for the declining number of available males is partially down to a higher death rate among men (after being more numerous at birth), but also it is due to the traditional preference of men to marry women younger than themselves.

For Christian women the problem is compounded by the shortage of male believers. Research by the UK Evangelical Alliance among its member churches showed that in the under-thirty age range, for every 100 single men there are 130 single women. (In the over-sixty age range it is 100 men to every 600 women.)

These are difficult figures and help to explain the intense pressures older Christian women feel to date non-Christians (an issue I deal with in a later chapter). But depression or panic dating is not a helpful response. For now, let me say that the church must have a strategy for dealing with its failure to convert men. And Christian women need to be very harsh on 'Christian' men who try to use the inequality of numbers to manipulate them into bed. Let me leave the theme for now by saying that the statistics make it clear that for a Christian woman there need to be strong countervailing arguments if she is to pursue a deliberate policy of delaying marriage. (For Christian men the statistics suggest that if they wait, their choice will improve. Perhaps this is another insight into the commitmentphobic Christian man.)

Paula is lovely – very bright, loads of common-sense, great wife material! At university she was chased by many eligible Christian men, but now in her mid-thirties the lack of suitable Christian men has meant she is currently dating a non-believer. The pressures of that include a less than understanding church which, as well as berating her for being spiritually 'unequally yoked', has suggested that this PhD woman should instead be intellectually unequally yoked by dating a garage mechanic in a nearby congregation. She is rueful about her naivety as a student and says: 'I thought that when Christian men went out of their way to walk me to a lecture or give me flowers they were just being friendly!'

Let us look in more detail at the reasons why both Christian men and women give more priority to their careers than to marriage. To them the choice appears to be between having a successful career or having a successful marriage. But is this a false conflict? Many husbands and wives are supportive of each other's careers, and show that by sharing the emotional and practical burdens. When the pressure is on at work, their partners find that they have support not hindrance at home. As the writer of Ecclesiastes puts it, 'Two is better than one, because they have a good return for their work. If one falls down his friend can lift him up. But pity the man who falls and has no-one to help him up!' (Unfortunately, few men have reached the point of seeing their wives' careers as being of equal importance to their own. The acid test of that would be to find out how many men would be willing to move their jobs to accommodate their wife's career.)

The other way in which getting married can benefit your career is if you are one of those many Christians who devote enormous amounts of thought-life to tracking down Mr or Miss Right. (That's probably most of us!) In that case getting married might be the best thing that happened to your career in terms of the emotional energy and time that would be liberated by not having to chase any more.

Another common reason we use to put off getting married is our need to get ourselves 'sorted out' first. But isn't a committed marriage the best place for a couple to help unload each other of the emotional baggage they've been carrying around? It strikes me, as I hurry through my thirties, that none of my single friends seems in danger of getting entirely sorted out on their own!

Getting married might be the best thing that happened to your career in terms of the emotional energy and time that would be liberated by not having to chase any more.

The fact that so many of our friends are leaving marriage until much later makes it easier for us to avoid examining our own reasons for delay. Just as 2,000 years ago Hebrew youth felt a huge pressure to get married before they were twenty, so we buy into our culture's norm for later marriage. But is this the right thing – for us or our children? What would a typical ten-year-old son prefer? A Mum and Dad who are in their early thirties or late forties? I know which are better at playing football! And, peering way into the next millennium, what about our grandchildren?

Would they like to have grandparents who are alive? For if you and I don't have children until we're forty, and then our children do the same, we would need to live to eighty to see our grandchildren.

And how long do we want to be married for? If you join the late marriage crowd, then the biggest risk to the two of you not celebrating your golden wedding anniversary is not divorce but death. There is a richness in some marriages which has taken decades of shared experiences to develop. A richness that our 'instant everything' generation finds hard to relate to.

How many of us have thought deeply about when is the ideal time to get hitched? For many of us men it is only when we realise that most of our friends have tied the knot – and we're left kicking our heels on a Saturday night – that we think, 'I must get married.' For women, the turning point can come when they see their girlfriend starting to send her children to school. Or when those nasty crow's feet appear in the mirror! Suddenly, from being cavalier about the process – 'If it happens, it happens' – we are propelled into a frantic search for a suitable partner. And as we all know, rushed jobs are often botched jobs.

A final thought courtesy of St Paul: 'It is better to marry than to burn with passion.' Very practical! If you, like so many of your brothers and sisters in the faith, find controlling your sexuality very difficult, then don't postpone marriage indefinitely. That's not to say you should marry the first person who comes along, but so many Christians blight their spiritual lives by immorality that for the 'burners' delaying marriage is not a wise strategy.

8
Sex

If you are anything like me you've probably flicked through to this chapter on sex first! (Indeed, you probably wouldn't have picked the book off the shelf if it didn't have sex in the title!) It is because of our society's fantastic obsession and pitiful failure with sex that we are so keen to read about it. For while we look forward to having sex, at the same time we realise that its wrong use can destroy the very relationships we are trying to form. Sometimes we have learned this through bitter personal experience. Chapter 9 focuses on redeeming the consequences of those failings – trying to ensure they don't mess up future relationships. But whether or not you've avoided those pitfalls in the past, this chapter looks to our future conduct as single Christians – seeking to place sex in perspective: as important but not all-important; as powerful but not impossible to control.

If we don't believe that we can control our sexuality, then we fall into one of two traps: we either excuse unholiness, saying, 'I couldn't help it,' or we avoid relationships because 'they always get sexual'. For not only is immorality breaking up romances, the fear of it is stopping a lot of relationships from forming. You and I have to stop believing that when men and women go out, things have to get very physical, very fast. It's a lie.

The rules we play by

As a teenager I was taught two key rules: first, don't take any clothes off, and secondly, don't touch anything that you haven't got. But it is amazing how ingenious lust is! While keeping entirely to the letter of these rules, we can manage to drive a coach and horses through the spirit of them. And here lies the problem. Because whatever rules on sexual conduct we have – and we all have our own rules – we will for ever be testing the boundaries, as well as pressing over the boundaries, if we don't have a holistic attitude to sex. Only when we fully understand the implications as well as the applications of sex, the people involved as well as the pleasure, will we start to have hearts as well as minds set on respecting our bodies.

Introducing the Campaign for Real Sex

Is there any physical thing that we can do which symbolises commitment more than sex? Is there anything which is more intimate than sex? No. For there is no greater physical expression of trust than two bodies uniting. We are hiding nothing – it is the most private revelation of ourselves that we can offer another person. We are giving all that we can to the other. Such commitment and disclosure are only justified by a deep relationship and only safe within its protection. It cannot be real sex if one or both parties reserve the right to reject the other the following day. That's why pre-marital sex can never be real sex.

Real sexual expression has something of heaven in it: two people who have committed themselves for all of their joint lives to each other before God, relaxed in each other's arms, knowing that the earthly security they have in each other rests itself in an eternal security in God. In the sexual act they are communicating. Communicating eternity, not transience. Communicating trust, not lust.

In such intimacy self-esteem is boosted because a person's partner has made them feel valued. Unlike pre-marital sex, real sex does not leave people feeling used and terribly alone. Real sex is not about my pleasure, my ecstasy, but yours. In real sex we both seek first and foremost our partner's pleasure. Our deep satisfaction is that we can rely on our partner to give, and we don't have to grasp.

That's not to pretend that all marital sex is wonderful. First sex is never an accomplished act. And when established married couples have difficulties in bed, the heart of the problem is often self-centredness. Real sex is never selfish.

The ways of our world

So that's a high view of sex as a precious gift from our Maker: a magnificent diamond that is best kept whole — shared with one person rather than smashed into dozens of pieces by dividing it with dozens of partners. Many non-Christians would agree with the ideal, but regard it as unrealistic. Since it is their thinking that surrounds us, let us start to unpack the world's view of sex and see the pressures that it places on us to give up on the ideal.

How good are you in bed?

As the Bond theme has it, 'Nobody does it better – makes me feel sad for the rest. Nobody does it half as good as you – baby, you're the best!'

Nobody? How does the singer (Carly Simon) know? If sexual technique and performance are your god, then maybe it's great to know that your current lover is top of the Football League. But do you have to sleep with the rest of the League to know that your current lover is the best? And what if they go off form? I guess they get relegated to sleeping on the sofa.

What marks would you award yourself for your performance between the sheets? Six out of ten for the pre-amble? Seven out of ten for sexual ecstasy? Eight out of ten for sound effects? It seems absurd, but this is the way so much of society judges sex. Good sex is marked by the quality of the momentary experience – not what went on before, or what goes on afterwards.

It is inevitable that when people compromise more and more on the amount of commitment that's needed to justify sexual intercourse, they will focus more on technique instead. My momentary high becomes my objective rather than whether sex has brought us closer together. If it's a one-night stand, then I might not remember your name, but I hope I remember the earth moving for me.

The tragedy of this pursuit of better sexual experiences – as witnessed from the Royal Family down to plebs like you and me – is that it does not work. Sex is much more than something we do for kicks. More than the buzz of an 'E' tablet. More than an anaesthetic to the pains of this life, clutching on to another person like an alcoholic clasps a bottle to temporarily blot out the world. And it's more than an attempt to hang on to someone who may not want to stay with us.

A short cut to commitment

When we're not using sex for kicks, then we're using it in an attempt to keep a relationship together. With our judgement often blurred by the experience of 'falling in love', we convince ourselves that sex will cement the relationship; that sex will lead to instant commitment. But the only thing that creates commitment is character. And character is often in short supply when we're indulging in pre-marital sex.

Here's the paradox: in sleeping with a person we hope it will add to their commitment to us, but in reality it does the reverse. Why? Well, in choosing a marriage partner we are looking for a strength of character and judgement that will last the years. Someone who will be emotionally and bodily faithful to us whatever the temptations. And any woman or man who is willing to sleep with you before marriage is in that very act demonstrating shallowness. We demonstrate our unreadiness for marriage by our willingness to go to bed. The morning after the night before we are

confused and our judgement is clouded. Sex too soon
has destabilised the very relationship that we hoped it
would preserve. So much is now at stake, precariously
balancing on top of a relationship that had not grown
to the point of being able to sustain it.

> **The only thing that creates commit-
> ment is character. And character is
> often in short supply when we're indul-
> ging in pre-marital sex.**

Your relationship is not made valid by having sex,
rather sex is made valid by the quality of your relationship. The more committed the relationship, the
more valid is the sexual activity – and there is no
more committed relationship than marriage. So
while an engaged couple who sleep together have a
sounder relationship than the proverbial 'one-night
stand', it is still not nearly as valid as those who have
publically declared the lifelong commitment of
marriage.

The only thing I have

But there is a deeper reason why our society rushes into
pre-marital sex. Which is that we are so lonely. Our
communities have fragmented. The extended family
has stretched to the point of non-communication. We
and our neighbours are too busy to talk to each other
and we even schedule our closest friends into next
month's diary because we can't find a mutually convenient date before then. The internet society is creat-

ing less and less time for face-to-face meetings. We are far less capable of building deep relationships than people were in our parents' generation. And the singleness that may have lasted only a few years for them can go on for decades for us.

The most common sickness of the 1990s is hug deprivation. I have a hot water bottle, but I would much prefer to be holding you.

So when in our swirl of busyness we meet someone who cares for us, we are desperate for their affection. And we will put up with a great deal – even compromising our beliefs on pre-marital sex – to end the loneliness. Especially as with the affection comes touch that feeds our emotional stomachs which have been crying out for closeness. The most common sickness of the 1990s is hug deprivation. I have a hot water bottle, but I would much prefer to be holding you.

Too late to be pure

Whether we've had pre-marital sex once, twice or a thousand times before, we know that we have broken the ideal. So why try to stick to the rules now? Well, foolishness yesterday doesn't make foolishness today any less foolish. Rather, every time a person breaks the rules it becomes even harder to turn back. You can get to the stage of being so highly sexually active that you ache, physically as well as emotionally, when you stop. Sex has become addictive, destructive sex which bounces your body from person to person with all the emotional commitment of a billiard ball. Such repetitive walk-away sex makes us feel even more hurt, more anaesthetised to our partner's humanity. If we don't stop this type of sex, then a real relationship and with it real sex becomes all but impossible.

Living together first

Cohabitation Defined

1. Type of compromise relationship designed by a man by which he can both have sex with a woman and get her to do his ironing without any commitment in return.

2. Psychological state in woman in which she deludes herself into believing that marriage is more likely if they live together first.

3. A trial marriage which turns out to be a trial not a marriage.

Is getting divorced your aim in life? Well, cohabit before marriage. National surveys in Britain, Sweden, the United States and Canada show that couples who live together before marriage are between 30 and 80 per cent more likely to get divorced than couples who didn't move in ahead of saying their vows. Partly it's down to one or both partners feeling trapped, and partly it is due to the initial lack of character shown by their willingness to live together

ahead of commitment remaining after they have tied
the knot. And that's only dealing with the cohabiting
relationships which do get as far as marriage. 'Common law' unions typically break down after two or
three years. The average marriage lasts just under
twenty-five years. No contest. What is tragic is that
so many women enter a cohabiting relationship with
the fervent desire that it will lead to a lasting marriage. Others see it as an essential way of testing his
suitability for marrying – of finding out what he is
really like. But a shrewd observation of a man's
character does not require sharing a bed with him.
Do that readily and he will take your sexual availability for granted.

**How can a woman, or a man, be totally
relaxed in a relationship which can be
dissolved simply by their partner walking out of the front door?**

In her book *Ten Stupid Things Women Do to
Mess up Their Lives*, Dr Laura Schlessinger
describes cohabitation as 'the ultimate female
self-delusion'. Is she too harsh? After all, there
are many cohabiting relationships where there is a
measure of genuine love and care. But how can a
woman, or a man, be totally relaxed in a relationship
which can be dissolved simply by their partner walking out of the front door? That really is a quickie
divorce. When a woman agrees to cohabitation (and
usually it is the man who is keener on the idea of

'pleasure without responsibility' than the woman) the fear of losing him is often high on her list of concerns. But is the relationship more likely to mature to the point where both parties are ready for commitment by cohabitation, or by living apart? Too often cohabitation becomes a stagnant relationship in which he is content but she isn't. And because he is satisfied there's no incentive for him to commit. He's already getting the best of both worlds.

The aim for women must be to restore the value of their sexual availability that was thrown away in the 'sexual liberation' of the 1960s. That devaluation of women's sexuality was dressed up in feminist rhetoric – that their sexual freedom showed that women weren't going to be shackled into the male-dominated institution of marriage. But instead it left women feeling more pressurised into having sex and thus less powerful in being able to demand tangible commitment in return.

So what are the Manufacturer's instructions?

If you think it's tough being pure in today's culture, just consider how difficult it was in biblical days. The local pagan religions had prostitutes in the temples, so you went to have sex as part of the worship. Wander around the ruins of Ephesus and you see the brothel slap in the middle of town. We, like the single Christians of first-century Ephesus and Corinth, are swimming against the tide. We have to be very clear in our thinking, as well as very determined, if we are going to shine like lights in this dark world. But let us be very confident that it is our view that has intellectual rigour – not the views of our secular friends, whose chief argument is, 'Well everybody else does it.'

Our choices in bed communicate respect or disrespect to both our partners and ourselves. And collectively these choices powerfully shape society. Societies which demean their bodies through repeated sex outside marriage create nations of insecure adults lacking a deep-rooted sense of self-worth. Insecure adults are unable to form deep relationships of trust. And where a man and woman do not trust each other in bed, they will not trust each other in the demanding task of building two-parent families.

This is why throughout Scripture there is a very strong emphasis on keeping sex within marriage. The Jews learned through experience, and their God taught through the prophets, that sexual immorality destroys societies – hence in Deuteronomy 22:13–30 the very strong penalities for pre-marital sex (the man having to marry the woman he had slept with, provide a dowry and, most significantly, be banned from ever divorcing her).

The New Testament is very tough on all sexual sin (*porneia* is the Greek – often translated as 'fornication'). While the apostle Paul does not treat sexual sin as uniquely awful, immorality was so prevalent in towns like Ephesus and Corinth that he repeatedly condemned it. Paul was particularly concerned about believers having sex with temple prostitutes, but let us not kid ourselves that he would have been any easier on our generation's tendency repeatedly to become 'one flesh' with a succession of partners.

How far should I go?

What would you like me to say – that groping is OK after the second date and that sleeping together is fine when you are engaged? Or should it be that holding hands is OK when you are serious, but the first kiss should be reserved until after the vicar has pronounced you man and wife? I don't want to say, 'This is in, but that is out,' because rules, on their own, just emphasise the negativity of sexual restraint and they tend to get ignored or circumvented. What I want to do is give you positive reasons for sexual restraint – ways to help you honour your body, your partner's body and your God.

The basic premise behind the 'How far should we go?' question is about setting outer limits on sexual contact before marriage. Why not turn the question on its head and ask: 'What is the minimum sexual involvement that is necessary for this relationship's emotional development?' The answer may be 'Remarkably little' because there are many excellent marriages where there was almost no physical involvement before the wedding. Obviously there is frustration in such restraint, but I would argue that it is less frustrating than the racing up to the precipice and then jamming on the brakes that is typical of unmarried Christian couples. And more important still, the respect that each partner is showing the other is enormously uplifting for the relationship. In short, it is not necessary or desirable to have any sexual caressing before marriage. Despite what our non-Christian friends say, just as we do not have to have sex before marriage, neither do we have to 'pet' or sexually stimulate our girl- or boyfriend. Before you dismiss that last sentence, I have a question for you. If you are currently going out with someone, which is more important – the relationship or the sexual activity? Which is more important – the relationship or the sexual activity? The repetition is not a printer's error. It is to urge you to think. Because whether it's a question of you pushing the boundaries, or whether you are the one being pushed to compromise on your standards, the relationship will suffer. Often it's because your partner will resent your attempts to pull them down to your standards. Even if you are not feeling confusion and guilt, they probably are. So don't be selfish towards the one you say you love.

In getting sexual you are sending out the message that you are not sure whether this relationship will last, so you are getting what you can from it now. We switch from being concerned about our partner's welfare (if we ever really were) to a 'let's enjoy it while it lasts' attitude. And a relationship in which one (or both) is being self-centred is in a downward spiral.

If you want your relationship to continue, then don't be so stupid as to risk a friendship that could offer a lifetime of happiness for the sake of an orgasm. You are showing yourself to be weak in self-control and character – not the best message to convey if you want your partner to consider you as future marriage material.

Decide now whether you are a giver or a taker; a person who builds others up or destroys them. For everything we do when we're going out either increases our partner's self-esteem or erodes it. Did we leave our last relationship feeling more confident about life or less? And what about our 'ex'? A common thread is that the more sexually involved we have been, the more bruised we are on breaking up.

If you want your relationship to continue, then don't be so stupid as to risk a friendship that could offer a lifetime of happiness for the sake of an orgasm.

And if the relationship is not one which you think could lead to a good marriage, what are you doing in it (let alone getting physical!) in the first place? Ask yourself, 'Is this lust or love?' I seem to remember love being defined as being 'patient, kind, not self-seeking, not delighting in evil'. And if you are one of the manipulative types who try to pressurise their partners into bed, just remember that you are at the same time aiming your soul at hell. If you don't believe me, try reading 1 Corinthians 6:9.

So next time the hands are wandering under the clothes, or fumbling with buttons, zips and fasteners, stop. Stop now because in a few seconds' time it will be even harder to cool down. Distract yourself from your ardour. Remember that you've got to phone your mother, feed the cat or put the dustbin out. Anything to help you flee from evil.

So now you really hate me! But just to show that I

am not completely insensitive, here is a concession. I think hugging is wonderful. Oh how we single people need to be hugged! Having long since left behind the hugs that parents, hopefully, gave us, there is often a great lack of touch in our lives. And who better to bestow hugs than a boy- or girlfriend? But let us be careful not to allow selfish lust to creep in amid the lengthy hugs. Our need for touch must not become an excuse for sexual indulgence.

Single Christians who are living holy lives are in a sexual desert. On finding the oasis of a relationship we are sorely tempted to gulp down sexuality to quench our sexual thirst, but we must find the self-control to sip with our lips, and savour the hors d'oeuvre of touch during courtship in order to enjoy the main course of sexuality after the wedding.

You struggle? So do I!

Let's get really practical. You are alone with your boy/girlfriend and the two of you are in a huggy mood. How do you stop a pleasant evening becoming a time you will regret later because you went further than you wanted? First of all set 'HTLs' or 'hugging time limits'. Take it from me – if a man and a woman are hugging each other, then just as a river will always flow downstream, one thing will lead to another. However good your intentions are, the longer you are hugging the more involved you will get. So be firm in your own resolve. When your HTL of, say, twenty minutes is over, get out of each other's arms and do something else. Anything! (Now if you can't really find anything else to do together that's fun apart from hugging each other, then I would gently suggest that the two of you are either very immature or deeply incompatible. The strength of a relationship is shown in the ability to communicate in a whole range of ways, the physical being just one aspect.)

When you are together, try to keep a clear distinction between what is a hug and what is sexual. If one of you says 'no' to something then the other must respect that. Don't try to push in that direction again a few moments later. Wearing down someone's resistance is not very Christian. And don't allow the past to affect the present. If five years ago or five minutes ago you were more physically involved than was wise, it does not mean that you have to do that or anything similar now. You may not respect what you did then, but now is the time to show you care for yourself by not using your body inappropriately. Saying 'no' demonstrates your self-confidence and respect. Don't allow yourself to think that the 'power' in the relationship is with the person who is pushing you further sexually. The power is with the person who says, 'Enough is enough.' If you are willing to end your relationship if your partner doesn't respect your body as much as you do, then they either have to come into line or get out of your life. So what do you do if your partner persistently refuses to respect your sexual limits? Ditch them. However much they may once have seemed the answer to your dreams, they are becoming a nightmare instead. What matters most is your walk with God, and getting excessively physical is going to mess that up.

Ten Ways to Be Sensible Tonight

1. Decide beforehand. What would you be happy explaining to God in tomorrow's quiet time?

2. Tell a wise Christian friend that you are tempted, and pray together.

3. Decide that you are not going to be influenced by either your or your partner's previous sexual history.

4. Decide that you are not going to fall for any rubbish lines like, 'If you loved me, you would want to show it.'

5. Be wise to the anxieties in your friend's life that are pushing him or her to go further than is appropriate.

6. Don't buy into the lie that being sexual will make your partner more committed. The opposite will happen.

7. Be very, very sensible about how much alcohol you drink.

8. Be wise to the effect that tiredness can also have on your judgement.

9. Don't go into bedrooms or any other place where you are tempted to lie down together.

10. Don't leave home without your self-respect, and make sure you bring it back with you.

'It's OK because we love each other'?

'But you don't understand,' I can hear you saying. 'We both love each other deeply and want to have sex, but we can't get married until we (a) have finished our degrees, (b) can afford the reception, (c) can get all the relatives together next year for the wedding!' Call me insensitive if you like, but I think such lines are third-rate excuses for immorality. If your relationship is not strong enough for marriage now, then it's not strong enough for sex now. If you, your friends and your pastor are convinced of the match but you are finding the self-control tough, then get married now. Better to have an inexpensive but genuine white wedding this year than a glitzy but hollow show next year. It's so daft to focus on the outward appearance instead of the inner reality.

If your relationship is not strong enough for marriage now, then it's not strong enough for sex now.

'But we really are getting married'

Fine: you are engaged, the wedding date is just a few months off and you are *still* not supposed to sleep with each other. For two people who are so very committed to each other, being told to stay out of bed is a cruel punishment. A prison sentence in which you are ticking off the days to that fateful Saturday when you are going to be pronounced man and wife. So why hold back?

One reason is because you have not burned your bridges until you are married. Until you have publically declared that the two of you are not looking for anyone else, your options are still open. I was engaged once, and I am glad that we did not sleep together – not least for the sake of the woman I may one day marry. For engagement is still a time of evaluation. Each of you still has the option to break off the relationship until you have said your vows. And the trouble with pre-marital sex is that it will cloud your judgement. The emotional bonding of sex, the sheer delight in each other's bodies, will stop you having that crucial last look before you leap into marriage. Take Kevin and Eileen, who are both Christians. They started having sex long before their wedding day. They did love each other, they were committed to each other and they did get married to each other, but blinded by sex, they did not realise that they were not as compatible as they thought until after they were married. Then in the day-to-day mundaneness of marriage this weakness in their friendship was exposed. They are now divorced. It doesn't always happen that way, but don't take the gamble.

Perhaps your desire to have pre-marital sex is a desire to test out the sexual side of the relationship before making a final decision to marry? What if you, as an engaged couple, have sex and find, as many do, that it is not initially as wonderful as you anticipated? Do you panic and split up? There is plenty of space and opportunity to seek counsel on perfecting the sexual side of the relationship after your wedding. But it's a bit awkward going up to your pastor before you get married to ask for advice on improving the sexual side of your relationship!

Another reason why pre-marital sex may be problematic (apart from sheer inexperience!) is that good sex is patient. It is also deeply thoughtful and respectful. Doesn't pre-marital sex, by its very nature, display an unwillingness to wait and a desire for each other's bodies above a desire for each other? My friends, it is best to wait those extra few months. After all, who wants to be pregnant going up the aisle?

Letter to my wife

Dearest Friend,

We haven't met yet, but I just wanted to explain what it will mean to me in the marriage service when I vow to 'honour you with my body'. It means that tonight, with the girlfriend I'm currently going out with, I will honour you by not letting my hands (or hers) wander where they shouldn't. It's a matter of respect – for you, her and me. It also means that when you and I start seeing each other, I'm going to control my passion for you, to avoid damaging your self-respect as well as your respect for me.

And finally, when we're married, it means that I will honour you with my body by speaking the language of sex to you, and you alone.

Yours,

Ian

9
Getting Really Personal

Sexuality is such an intensely private matter that it is often difficult to discuss all our concerns – even with close friends. And given that some of our sexual backgrounds have been anything but the Christian ideal, there are some issues which are simply never aired. Instead they just buzz around our minds.

Starting with the pressures facing those who have never had sex, I hope the next few pages are of help.

Virgin on the ridiculous

'Unless you have had sex, you're not a real man or woman. You are incomplete, uninitiated and in some ways immature.' What complete rubbish! But this is the implication of current attitudes. Those who have not had sex are seen as not being fully adult. Whether it's from teenage magazines encouraging their readers to have under-aged sex because everyone else is doing it, or television programmes mocking adults who have chosen to be celibate, there is a huge pressure to go with the flow.

Having sex does not need much ability. The physical act does not require us to exert the higher limits of our human abilities. After all, birds do it, bees do it (so they say, but I don't know how!), even cats and dogs do it. Humans are not mystically extended by the simple performance of the sexual act. Our humanity, our distinction from the animal kingdom, is shown in our ability to restrain our sexuality, to channel it into relationships – not to mate with everything that moves. Promiscuous sex diminishes us.

But our perverse generation has managed to turn the self-control of virginity into a symbol of ridicule. Being a virgin is not seen as a badge of honour, but as a mark of being undesirable. To many British youth, the word primarily conjures up notions of a hip record company rather than notions of honour and trust. The word 'celibate' isn't much better; the failings of many Roman Catholic priests to bear the burden of lifelong chastity risk turning the word into a synonym for hypocrisy. But since we need a phrase to describe those who haven't had sex, what about 'sexually honest'? It sums up the attitude of those who are not prepared to lie with their bodies; not prepared to say with their bodies that they are committed to a person when they – or the other person – are not.

Those of us who have disciplined ourselves away from pre-marital sex should not be bitter about what we have missed out on, because those who have indulged know that sex without commitment equals pain. The painful path has been trodden by so many: the flattery, alcohol, loneliness or desperation that first got them into bed; the falling in love and the longing that commitment will follow the sex; the tears when it doesn't. It is an iron law of creation that sex outside a committed, long-term relationship is always destructive.

Male hypocrisy

The discussion of such 'sexual honesty' brings us neatly to the topic of male hypocrisy. 'Men do, so why shouldn't we?' was the clarion cry of women in the 1960s. Emboldened by the pill, they set about a game of catch up. But not only has such freedom cost women dearly emotionally, it has played into the hands of those men who delight in sex without strings. There is no shot-gun these days to say that because you slept with her you should be prepared to marry her. And if she becomes pregnant – well, that is her fault for not having used the pill. Your only responsibility is to send her a get-well card after the abortion. This is not sexual heaven, but the freedom of hell.

Not all men are such heartless hypocrites. Not all expect to marry a chaste woman regardless of their own history. Some men do not regard their wives' bodies as their own property. But there is a biological insight which may help women understand why men can be hypersensitive to 'their' woman having slept with someone else. The 'Parental Investment Hypothesis' is based on the assumption that we all want to pass on our genes to the next generation. While a man can, in theory, father countless children, a woman is limited by a narrower band of fertile years and the nine-month gestation cycle. For a woman the danger is that the man will desert her after she has conceived his child. For a man the risk is that the woman will try to pass off a child conceived through sex with another man as his offspring. Without wishing to place too much weight on this theory, it does give a plausible explanation for men's sexual jealousy and women's emotional jealousy. The 'neural circuitry' that has evolved in our heads makes women intensely concerned about their men's emotional loyalty and men about their wives' physical fidelity.

Sexual purity is much more than a physical state. It is a declaration of vision, a demonstration of character and an example of wise judgement.

My partner has, but I haven't

Sexual sin offends God because he sees how much we hurt ourselves and others by stepping outside his guidelines. While Christians know that God forgives all our sins, our sexual sins have a habit of continuing to haunt us – not least in a new relationship where one partner has a 'history' and the other hasn't. The 'guilty' party has often dealt with the issue before God and finds it hard to understand why their boy- or girlfriend struggles to forgive. Sadly, promising relationships can fall unnecessarily at this hurdle – relationships that could have become excellent marriages. If we are to be reconciled to each other, we need first to disentangle a little theology.

To begin with, God does forgive those who renounce sexual sin. 'Though your sins are like scarlet, they shall be as white as snow' is Isaiah's marvellous imagery of the complete way in which God forgives our sins. This is the most critical forgiveness in that it enables us to be reconciled to our Creator. And another 'yes'! There is indeed a difference between those who knew that sexual sin was wrong yet still indulged, and those who in ignorance went along with the practice of the age to treat intercourse more casually than their parents took kissing. But even where we acted in ignorance, and even though we have confidence that we now stand before God clothed in the righteousness of Jesus (the only way anyone can stand before God), we still have to face the consequences of our actions. Repentance opens up our relationship with our Creator and persuades us from further damaging his creation. It gives us the opportunity to rebuild, but it does not instantly repair all that we have damaged.

The cross and the past

Tonight at church I did something I rarely do. I sat on the front row, bang in the middle (normally it's anonymously behind the pillar on row fourteen so the preacher can't see me filling in next week's diary during the sermon). Anyway, after the talk a big wooden cross was brought to the centre of the platform, straight in front of me. And for the next half hour I looked at this thing, which was about twelve feet high. I think it was 'meant' because I'd been aware of some past sin. How could I have been so thoughtless? After all the years I had been a Christian, how could I have been so stupid? My heart was full of anguish, my mind loaded with anger at myself. How could God forgive me? Well, the answer was staring down in front of me. And since by thought, word or deed all of us sin sexually – to one degree or another – this prayer is for you as well as for me.

A prayer

Father, forgive our foolishness. Forgive us for the pain that we have caused you, as well as others and ourselves. All your ways are perfect and yet we have gone off on our own path, messing up your creation. Help us to understand the grief our sin causes you so that we will never be so stupid again. We are responsible for our sin. Yet as we see the scale of what we have done, help us to look up at the cross that towers over us, and to see that its love is far, far greater than our sin. Help us to leave our sin there, and not to pick it up again day after day. Jesus died to give us a fresh start, so help us, Father, to honour his sacrifice by leaving the past behind, and to see that since we have been forgiven so much, we should love you much in return. Amen.

The reasons we stay pure

In today's deeply immoral society we have to be something of a fanatic to stay sexually honest. A person who is living a celibate lifestyle has repeat-edly justified their sexual self-denial to themselves on a number of grounds. There are the physical factors – avoiding the pitfalls of unwanted pregnan-cies and sexually transmitted diseases – then there are the emotional reasons – sexual intercourse being the most intimate of acts is saved for the most committed of relationships. Promiscuous sex, the chaste rightly convince themselves, debases sex and erodes the self-respect of those who indulge. Then there is the intellectual assessment: a person who doesn't 'save' themselves for marriage is more likely to commit adultery than someone who has been sexually disciplined. And there is the fear that whether consciously or not, the non-virgin will compare the sexual performance of a marriage partner with that of previous lovers. And for the spouse who has a 'history', memories of pre-marital sex can haunt the marital act. Add all that to the spiritual dynamic in which the Bible talks about intercourse making us 'one flesh', and the celibate Christian has developed a formidable mental armoury of reasons why sex outside marriage should be avoided at all costs. So if someone comes into their life who has not played by the rules, then that person's past value system appears to mock the discipline of the celibate partner.

There is therefore a recipe for mistrust that preys on the minds of the sexually honest where their partner has a sexual history. Has he got syphilis or HIV? Why should we be restrained during courtship when she has given herself completely to other men in the past? Is there something in his character which is going to make him head off with other women when I'm pregnant? Is she still 'one flesh' with the guys she slept with? Each of these thoughts needs working through, either together or with a pastor. Trust can only be established where both parties take the time to seek to understand each other.

When two people who have stayed sexually honest meet up, their previous disciplined conduct straight away provides a substantial amount of mutual respect and trust in each other. But this brick wall of trust is damaged every time a person has sex outside marriage. Even when you have found complete forgiveness before God, the brick wall of trust still needs to be rebuilt. And what rebuilds it? Every month and every year that you stay sexually honest shows a future potential spouse your integrity. It is not about trying to become a 'born-again virgin', but about demonstrating character.

This rebuilding takes time and patience. What is utterly unhelpful is for those who are virgins to use their moral purity as a justification for self-righteous judging. Without the humility to see that moral failure could so easily have been their experience, they risk becoming Pharisees. And Pharisees are deeply unattractive people.

Forgiveness and trust

What I am trying to do is to draw a distinction between forgiveness and trust. When a person comes to the cross and begins to understand the full measure of the suffering of Jesus, then they will not see their own sin or that of their partner as beyond the forgiveness of God. No one has a right to condemn those whom God has forgiven because to do so is to challenge the authority of heaven.

But trust is a choice. Whether it is a wife's adultery or a boyfriend's previous promiscuous lifestyle, we are obliged to forgive as God forgave us. That is his divine command that frees us from bitterness. But there is no obligation to trust again. It is often in our interest to trust, but it is for us to choose.

Private agony

Turning now from our struggles with each other, we look at our struggles with ourselves, and in particular a subject that causes Christians immense amounts of anxiety but should never be mentioned at a vicar's tea party (that is unless you want to see everyone's faces go red and the minister to look more steamed up than the kettle). We are of course talking about that hypersensitive subject, masturbation.

When the vicar has forgiven you for causing everyone to drop his best bone china out of shock, you may not be in line for that much in the way of helpful advice on the subject. You may get some obscure reference from the Book of Genesis about the alleged sins of some fellow called Onan and, if you are deeply unlucky, some advice about 'plucking your eye out'! The trouble is that the authors of the Bible didn't get hot under the collar about masturbation.

They didn't need to – they nearly all got married before they were twenty. So Bible scholars trying to get heavy about masturbation are fumbling in the dark – if you'll pardon the expression.

Well, if the Bible isn't exactly loaded with heavy-duty denunciations of masturbation then it must be completely fine. Steady on, not so fast! I do think that the biggest problem with masturbation is how much we worry about it. (Now 'worry' is something the Bible is very clearly against.) The huge guilt trips some of us go on must have the devil laughing himself silly. I have even come across guys who stopped going to church because they felt so guilty about masturbation. Be real. If we're lonely, tired, depressed or feeling sexually frustrated most us will masturbate. Women as well as men. A recent survey among American Christians put it at 75 per cent. So if everyone who masturbated didn't turn up for church, the attendance figures wouldn't be too hot.

We have to recognise the difference between 'condemnation' – where we're plagued with a blanket sense of unworthiness before God and our fellow Christians – and 'conviction', which comes from the Holy Spirit. The latter is very specific and very practical. Its aim is to get us straight back into close relationship with God, determined to avoid sin in the future. So please, please don't get so worked up about this issue that it undermines your relationship with God.

Staying very practical, what about our sexual appetite – the huge tensions that can build up which cry out for some type of outlet? This is difficult for the long-term Christian single, and incredibly tough for the recent convert who's just come out of a physical relationship. First, it is far better to masturbate than to get into bed with someone you are not married to, with all the destructive physical, emotional and spiritual consequences that can have. But your long-term aim must be to become gradually more and more in control of your sexuality. And if you are addicted to masturbation – say if you couldn't completely stop for a week – then you are not really in charge of your sexuality. Learn to control your sex drive now and you will be learning to become a better lover when you are married, for making love as opposed to taking love is about patience and caring. Far too often our sexual fantasies are about seizing our own gratification. They are not focused on what might one day please a potential spouse. Let us be cautious about the way masturbation can result in a mindset of self-centredness. We must not deny the reality that we have been made sexual beings, because that is repression, but equally let us not foster selfish sexual thought patterns that will be unhelpful in marriage.

My biggest hang-up about masturbation is that it is such a waste of time. There are a thousand and one different things we could get on with rather than lying in bed masturbating. Like deciding to phone up a member of the opposite sex to ask them out for a date. Now that's focusing on reality – trying to form real friendships rather than pretend ones in your mind. Much more satisfying. And what about God? When you are at that moment of loneliness and sexual frustration where you would normally masturbate, why not, for a change, focus on your Creator and talk to him in your hour of need? Discuss with God the type of partner you are after, and urge him to hurry up!

Finally, if the vicar is being all heavy about masturbation, despite his being tucked up with his wife every night, ask him a fair question: How many times"did he masturbate before he got married?

If looks could kill

If masturbation is not a great topic for the vicar's tea party, try telling him that you have a problem with pornography and he'll choke on his sandwich. My sympathy is with the vicar on this one. I mean, it's not a pretty sight for God, looking down from heaven on one of his sons getting sweaty over a picture (and it's usually guys doing this as very few women have a problem with pornography). Like masturbation, pornography is a quick fix for sexual frustration. But while masturbation sometimes chains people up in lustful thought patterns, pornography is far more addictive. And like any hard drug, the more you use the more you need. The pictures get more depraved. You get more trapped. With masturbation the message is 'less is better'. With pornography it is 'stop completely'. Although for most men who've got chained up with pornography the outlook is very bleak, we sons of the living God have access to the bulk cutters of prayer. So when you are fed up with being fed up, go back to the vicar. Apologise for teasing him about masturbation, and ask him to pray you into the freedom that is God's purpose for all his sons. It may take a few sessions until you are 'free indeed', but if you persist with pornography then you are heading for a spiritual crash. Confession is the key. Then burn all the porn and flee from all temptation.

If you are a man who has a girlfriend, then your parallel use of pornography will provoke all manner of guilt, shame and self-disgust. You won't be able to stop looking at her with 'x-ray eyes', and you'll either find yourself wanting inappropriate intimacy or being fearful of all intimacy.

Sexual fantasy also ruins honeymoons, for whether you've been fantasising about your girlfriend through pornography or masturbation, the images in your mind will be out of kilter with the tender, caring reality that is needed.

Gay but not gay

This chapter hasn't been shy of some of the toughest issues in sexuality. Yet difficult as these issues are, a bigger sexual trauma is for those struggling with their orientation. There must be compassion and empathy for those who are the rope in the tug-of-war between ferociously aggressive gay proselytisers and the hell-fire brigade on the Christian right wing.

I don't think I've ever heard a rational debate on homosexuality. The issue is so polarised that whenever the two views do meet things usually degenerate

into a slanging match. Amid that din, and the powerful pleadings of their sex drive, it is very hard for a
man or woman to work out whether or not they are
homosexual. And whether or not that is God's inten-
tion for the remainder of their life.

My scientist friends tell me that while the evidence
over what causes homosexual tendencies is fragmented, every scrap is fought over because of the implications. For if genetic studies were to prove that
homosexuality was primarily inherited, then it
would be hard to argue that being gay was not at
least in part biologically normal. And scientific
studies of enlarged hypothalamus glands, identical
twins and Xq28 genes do suggest that homosexuality
does have some genetic roots. But the evidence is
pointing to genes contributing to a tendency for
some people to be attracted to their own gender.
Contributing to a tendency, not compelling someone. Genes do not determine someone's orientation
– that is still the choice, and hence also the responsibility, of the individual.

Combined with the genetic influence is the psychological aspect. Our childhood has a powerful
impact on our sexual orientation. Common backgrounds among homosexuals include over-dominant
mothers, absent fathers or sexual abuse by a family
member or neighbour.

If an adolescent has a genetic and/or psychological
background making them at all uncertain about their
sexual orientation, then this ambiguity over sexual
orientation is often picked up by older homosexuals,
and if an affair ensues the initial tendency is rein-

forced by sexual experience. Our first sexual experiences are printed deeply on our psyche.

But whatever the particular pot pourri of influences that has led to a man or woman having an aversion to the opposite sex, how are they supposed to live now that they have that orientation? Especially if they love a God who, as Scripture indicates, designed sexual activity solely for man–woman relationships? I agree with those who argue that God did not physically design us for homosexuality. And there is a strong argument in that the biological survival and social stability of society are not helped by having a large pool of men pairing off with each other. It is not much help for heterosexual women.

What I cannot abide, however, are the utterly crass comments older Christians make to those caught up in this struggle. I despair for those who have effectively been driven from the church into the difficulties of living in the homosexual community by believers castigating them. Whether this rejection is motivated by fear or an Old Testament style of legalism, it does not reflect the grace and love of God.

How not to treat homosexuals

Take Ed, for example (not his real name, but you understand why I've changed it). He grew up in an evangelical home in England and had become enthusiastic about his faith. As a teenager Ed had felt uncertain over his sexual orientation but had not shared his doubts with his parents, sisters or friends. At university his homosexuality became active, but still it was hidden from those who knew him best. It was only later in his early twenties that a bizarre set of circumstances led to his two closest Christian friends discovering that he was gay. For reasons which are still not clear, they felt obliged to write to Ed's parents telling them of their son's homosexuality. The impact of this breach of confidence was huge distress for his parents – his mother was distraught, blaming herself for her son's sexuality – and Ed left the evangelical church he had been attending, although for a number of years he continued going to another church. He is no longer attending church, although he does still have a faith and a love for God. He doesn't have a partner and speaks of his fears of growing old 'with no one there for me'.

> **If a man is a believer and gay, then he is my brother in Christ first and a homosexual second. That does not mean I approve of his homosexual practice – I see that as a trap – but he is still my brother.**

Let me be blunt. If a man is a believer and gay, then he is my brother in Christ first and a homosexual second. That does not mean I approve of his homosexual practice – I see that as a trap – but he is still my brother. My concern is how, starting where he is now, he can be drawn closer to God. If you, my reader, are in these shoes and torn between your faith and your sexuality, then I beg you not to give up on your desire to know the God of all compassion better. Instead I urge you to seek out the wisest, most loving, most spiritual Christian counsellors you can find; people you can trust to respect your privacy as you work out the conflict within you.

A few other general points. First, our sexuality is not the central aspect of our lives. Hetero- and homosexually orientated people need to live as if they are more than life-support systems for their genitalia. Yes, your homosexual drive may be strong, but so is my heterosexual drive. And in twenty years of being highly aware of that sex drive I have been sexually disciplined. Celibacy is tough, but the alternative of destructive sex is not worthwhile.

Secondly, be careful of your relations with women. Unless they are aware of your homosexuality they may find your friendliness and lack of sexual predatoriness a highly attractive combination. While you may not wish to disclose your sexuality, make sure that your female friends are not left with unreal expectations.

Finally, God is much, much bigger than our problems; much, much more caring than the greatest lover. And utterly committed to our living fulfilled lives. So surrender your life to him and ask your Creator to put you in alignment with the person he created you to be. This is as true for lesbians as it is for gay men.

I've never been able to tell anyone this before . . .

The above catalogue of sexual complications experienced by Christians is far from exhaustive. It is horrific that more believers than we care to imagine have got into utter bondage because they've been involved in practices such as sado-masochism, three-in-a-bed sex, bestiality or perpetrating paedophilia. God knows how long the list is. And only he knows how many decades people can be spiritually locked up in their degradation and shame; isolated, feeling trapped with no hope of escape.

If you look hard enough you will find that there are Christian counsellors who will not be shocked. They have privately led so many to the freedom of laying their burdens at the foot of the cross. Whatever the depths of wickedness, the love and forgiveness God has made available through Jesus' death are far, far deeper. Whatever your load of sexual sin, Jesus offers to carry it. So give it to him and he will lift both the emotional and mental burden. And over time he can and will help you break the behaviour patterns as well.

10
Quitting Fantasyland

Our church youth group had spent the night sleeping in St James's Park in central London. We got up early to make sure we had a good view. And then, after several hours of waiting, we saw for a few brief seconds what we had been waiting for: a gilded carriage taking Lady Diana to St Paul's Cathedral. The Prince had found his Princess. And in a ceremony that fulfilled both childhood fables and Hollywood romantic films, they became man and wife. It was so obviously meant to be. They would live happily ever after. In an age of uncertainty we had found something we could believe in.

How our fantasy has been shattered! The ensuing saga of betrayal and bitterness has left the world's most photographed woman emotionally battered and our future king a target of scorn. And fantasies about marital bliss have turned into cynicism. Why go through the living hell of an awful marriage when you can be unhappily single instead? In short, marriage is for mugs.

We slip so easily between such fantasy and cynicism because they are both founded on shallow thinking. One view says that a marriage is bound

130

to succeed, the other that it is bound to fail. Neither encourages us to think carefully about our choice of partner. Neither encourages us to invest the hard work and commitment that are necessary for a marriage to work. If we are not willing to make the effort to be realists we will always be rocked back and forth between fantasy and cynicism – wanting to believe in the fairytale, but bitterly disillusioned every time we see a marriage failing.

When it comes to shallow thinking Christians seem to specialise in fantasy. In this chapter I'm about to take careful aim at some of your fantasies . . . and pull the trigger.

Fantasy number one: 'Falling in love shows that I've met the right person'

The year is 1990, and I'm living in Switzerland. Her name is Marieke, she's a woman of God, doing a PhD at a local university, and very pretty. And what's more, a mutual friend has told me that Marieke is keen on me. Suddenly the world seems a very wonderful place. The woman for my life has arrived in my life. The years of waiting are over, the years ahead are certain. Oh the ecstasy! But my friend has made a mistake and Marieke tells me there is a man in her native South Africa whom she is still fond of. Ah the agony! Now there are storm clouds overhead and a churning sea of emotions in my heart. Whatever my Job's comforters say to me cannot soothe my hurt.

Only after that rollercoaster ride of falling in love was over did a few realities become clear. First, while

the experience of falling in love had made me feel
that Marieke and I were destined for each other, for
ever, we were not really suited. She had a cultural
background very different from mine and our per-
sonalities and interests didn't match that well. Secondly, while my emotions towards Marieke were very
intense, they were in reality selfishness dressed up as
love. I was wrapped up in what Marieke would mean
for me, not in how I could serve and care for her.
Infatuation is not as cosy a term as 'falling in love',
but that is what it was.

I was lucky. While I can now laugh at the memory of
those mad summer days, for many Christians the
aftermath of falling in love can be the agony of trying
to save a marriage to someone they are not very compatible with. It happens so easily: Arthur and Abigail
go to Terry's party. Arthur thinks Abigail is sexy and
has been eyeing her up all evening. Abigail (who,
being a woman, has been much more subtly assessing
the men at the party) has come to the conclusion that
Arthur looks cute. So when Arthur asks her to dance
she's not saying 'no'. A quick kiss and a cuddle and the
motor of falling in love starts to rev up. The combination of physical contact and emotional infatuation
can leave Arthur and Abigail quickly feeling deeply
committed to each other. They justify their relationship to themselves and their friends by saying that
they've fallen in love. Only later, when the infatuation
fades, do they start to look at how compatible they
really are with each other. But it may be too late. The
only thing that Arthur and Abigail may have in
common is that initially they both found each other

physically attractive. The painful truth is that, as in secular society, relationships in the church are often founded on the most shallow of initial attractions.

Those who avoid marrying someone with whom they are not compatible can still be scarred by the illusions of falling in love. The report 'Sexual Behaviour in Britain' showed that 40 per cent of girls who first had sex under the age of sixteen said they were in love at the time. Only 6 per cent of boys gave the same explanation.

There is a galaxy of difference between the essentially self-centred experience of falling in love and the other-centredness of committed love that actually holds relationships together.

It is romantic heresy to say it, but that glorious feeling known as falling in love is no guide to a couple's compatibility. We can fall in love with the most unsuitable people. There is a galaxy of difference between the essentially self-centred experience of falling in love and the other-centredness of committed love that actually holds relationships together.

If falling in love can lead to so much woe, what is causing it? In his classic book *The Road Less Travelled*, the American psychiatrist M. Scott Peck describes falling in love as a psychological ploy of mother nature designed to get us to mate. 'To serve as effectively as it does to trap us into marriage,' he says, 'the experience of falling in love probably must have as one of its characteristics the illusion that the experience will last forever.'

Mother nature is not interested in whether we have found a compatible friend for life – just in encouraging us to have sex and pass on our genes to the next generation. And falling in love is always a temporary phenomenon, albeit one that gives us plenty of encouragement to indulge in unwise sex.

To Scott Peck the delicious feeling of falling in love is not only a transient phase, but also a regression to a childlike stage where the world revolves around us. It convinces us that we and our beloved are one; that we will never again be alone in this unfriendly world. Unfortunately, we wake up to find that the other party does not do exactly what we want, that they are a different personality. And so we 'fall out of love'.

Some couples who have been married for decades do say that they have been 'in love' throughout their marriage, but this is a form of words. They are not saying that they have been in the midst of the intensely emotionally draining phase of 'falling in love' all that time. Rather they are saying that they have always been deeply committed and full of delight in each other.

Falling in love mimics real love, but in reality it is almost the reverse of real love. Whereas real love is a choice, falling in love is an involuntary infatuation. While selfless love is other-centred, falling in love is focused on satisfying our own needs. We can't help feeling the powerful emotion of falling in love, but we can and must control our behaviour during this temporary phase. If we don't, we will find that we've made some disastrous decisions.

Fantasy number two: 'There is only one person meant for me'

The Siamese twin of falling in love is the belief that there is only one person meant for each of us. Since falling in love convinces us that our match is perfect, we assume the two of us will satisfy all of each other's needs for ever. When it transpires that we don't, the infatuation fades, and we're horrified that we must have made a dreadful mistake and married the wrong person. Scott Peck says that at this point, the romantic myth of falling in love suggests that 'nothing can be done about the situation than to live unhappily ever after or get divorced'. In short, this psychiatrist's verdict is that 'the myth of romantic love is a dreadful lie'. Another American writer on relationships, Barbara DeAngelis, regards the 'one person' belief as a sign of emotional immaturity and unreadiness for marriage.

So why do we so tenaciously hold onto this 'lie'? Why do we insist to ourselves that there is only one person meant for us? It is because when our head is whispering, 'Be cautious,' we're not simply contending with mother nature screaming at us, 'This is the one you've been looking for.' Added to this power of biology is the forceful influence of our culture.

Secular culture

'*And they all lived happily ever after.*' Look through the romantic storylines of childhood fables, the slushy lyrics of pop songs, the plot of a movie, or the formula of a Mills and Boon novel, and you will find a common belief. The conviction that there is someone out there whom you are destined to meet. Keep a count this week of just how many times you come across this message of people being meant for each other – in poems, advertisements, television chat shows. You'll see how relentlessly the belief is fed to us.

Christian culture

'*Alone and blue? Here's what to do. Join Made For Each Other Christian Introductions. And getta betta life.*' This recent advertisement in a British magazine for a Christian dating agency is just one example of how the notion that there is someone meant just for you has spread into Christian thinking. Many married couples are sincerely convinced that they are married to heaven's intended. And there are more than a few church ministers who take this line as well. They counsel their singles only ever to go out with one person: their future spouse whom God will point out to them before they start dating each other.

So our biology and our culture seek to convince us that there is only one person for us. So what's wrong – and what's right – with this view? It does seem very natural for Christians who put God at the centre of their lives to want to be guided by him on such a critical decision as the choice of a marriage partner. And having heard from God we have confidence to take the awe-inspiring decision to commit the rest of our lives to one partner. A person who will help us raise a Christian family.

But there are plenty of pitfalls with this view. Not least of which is the difficulty of hearing clearly from God if we are either 'under the influence' of having fallen in love, or we are desperate to get married. I have a delightful Christian friend who, in the space of weeks, had two men come up to her at church and tell her: 'God has told me that we should get married.' Some chat-up line! Now my theology indicates that at least one of the men was wrong. My instinct suggests that both were living in fantasyland.

My friend sent these men packing. Hopefully they got some counselling because people who start spiritualising their desires in this way need to be helped towards reality, otherwise they keep on hurting themselves as well as their 'targets'. For what happens when the object of the approach is equally desperate to believe that God is approving the relationship? We need to use the mind that God has given us to assess relationships rather than 'use' God to justify what objectively may be pretty ropey matches. It's not unbiblical to think.

At the heart of the issue is the attitude that thinking a decision through is somehow unspiritual. 'Pray, but don't think' seems to be the motto for Christians who effectively deny that it is God who created our minds, and God who, since our conversion, has been renewing them. These minds should be allowed to think long and hard about the suitability of a partner, even if it may seem more 'religious' to rely on a verse justifying what we are doing. This is not to deny the marvellous ways in which many have clearly seen God encourage them to marry, but these are often Christian couples who have over the years become well used to hearing from their supernatural Father in heaven. Many other younger Christians try to mimic this mature spirituality.

What we are doing in looking for confirmation is often more akin to religious magic – asking God to act as a water diviner's rod, guiding us towards a particular partner. We've all done it! After we've been praying about marriage we convince ourselves that God will bring the right person to sit down next to us at church that evening. Then we find the person next to us is thirty years older, and already married! We are trying to pass the buck for a hugely important decision of marriage that ultimately only we can and should take. Sometimes there are people only too ready to take over our responsibility.

Take, for example, Peter and Marie. They met eighteen months ago and despite it having been a very turbulent relationship they are still very much in love with each other. They both would like to marry, yet Peter has some (quite proper) cautions. Enter two older Christians, Mark and Rachel, who are both strongly advising Peter not to marry Marie. So strongly that they are dressing up their advice by saying that God does not approve of the match. This, despite the fact that Mark has never met Marie, and Rachel has only seen her once.

It is so easy for our Christian faith to become one big dependency culture in which those who are psychologically inclined to give advice dispense it to those who are inclined to receive it. Nowhere more so than over such an awesome decision like who to marry. It is very comforting to have our decision, whether it be 'yes' or 'no', confirmed by God. But have we or our advisers really heard from God, or are we simply spiritualising our feelings? As a brand new baby Christian of seventeen, I remember being heartbroken when I was told by a girl I had just started dating that God had told her not to go out with me. My anguish, however, was not so much about her (I hardly knew her), it was about how God could be so beastly. Later, I realised that it was simply the case that this girl had (for some inexplicable reason) decided that I was no longer her cup of tea, but she was not willing to take responsibility for her decision. Let us now move up the age range to the case of Sandra.

Sandra is very intense about her faith. Unfortunately she was also rather too intense about a boyfriend a few years ago. She had sex with him on a regular basis, despite feeling very condemned about it. Now she is petrified that things could go the same way with her current boyfriend. Instead of specifically confronting her past failings and her future fears, she is avoiding them by saying that God has told her that she should split up with her current boyfriend – he is not 'the one' for her. This is despite the fact that both of them feel very strongly for each other, and seem to outsiders to be very well matched.

I have no qualms about Christians speaking 'as from God' to individuals who are clearly in breach of the word of God. But on a question like who to go out with, or who to marry, we should be very, very sure before we suggest that we have heard directly and undiluted from heaven. After all, in the marriage service the words are 'I will' rather than 'God has told me'.

Sometimes God does speak clearly to people about who to marry. However, that is not always the case and it certainly does not make a relationship inherently less godly if the couple did not feel so directly guided to each other. Indeed a marriage brought together by God can still fail. The husband and wife each have free will to rebel against God and to stop loving each other. Whether or not God has one person, and one person only, intended for us should not be used as cover to evade responsibility for our decisions.

Our view on the 'one person' issue is moulded by our overall view of God. Some think that if we step off the very narrow pathway that he has for our lives, then we have irreversibly blown it. Others take the line that while the Lord is our Shepherd and guides us to green pastures, he doesn't tell us which blade of grass to eat, although he will warn us if we are straying off the path and in danger of being eaten up by a wolf.

Nowhere in scripture does it say that there is only one person meant for you. (Vera Sinton, Lecturer at Wycliffe Hall in Oxford and a speaker on singleness)

Scripture does not speak much about how we are to choose our partner. The Bible was written among cultures in which arranged marriages were the norm. Proverbs 31 talks about 'finding a wife', and Paul in 1 Corinthians 7 speaks of 'looking for a wife', but neither talks about locating *the* one woman or man for your life.

It is the institution of marriage that has been

designed by our Creator and it is his gift to us all, to use well or badly. He has provided the shoe-box, and we are one of the shoes. But it is for us to find the other shoe! If we hold the view that there is only one person for us then we will always be scared of marrying 'the wrong person'. We will find our search for a partner dominated by fear instead of faith.

Fantasy number three: 'My partner will be perfect'

We've waited so long for Mr or Miss Right to come along that they had better be good! And if we think the decision on who we are to marry has been made in the throne room of heaven it stands to reason that this will be the most perfect of matches. This simplistic theology dovetails neatly with our consumer culture that insists we should demand the very best.

The Christian tendency to hang on for the mythical perfect partner helps explain why so many of us are unmarried.

It is a very alluring theory, especially for those trying to escape the risk of entering a marriage which ends in divorce, but by definition, most of us are average. So we are deluding ourselves if we focus only on potential partners who fit our exacting checklist. They must be emotionally secure, good-looking, intelligent, well off and possess an intense passion for housework! Even though we may score pretty low by our own yardsticks we expect them to show interest in us. The Christian tendency to hang on for the mythical perfect partner helps explain why so many of us are unmarried.

The burden of Scripture doesn't focus on finding *the* perfect partner for our lives. Our prayers should instead start by acknowledging that it is us who God tells to 'be perfect'. We need to ask God to uncover the unlovely parts of our characters that we like to hide and to ask him to change us. We need to confess our anxiety about marriage for the sin it is, and ask him to replace our worries with a joyful confidence in his provision. He may parachute someone into our lives, or he may want us to do some of the looking ourselves. But whatever we do, we must do it with faith that God delights in men and women developing friendships.

Fantasy number four: 'We're destined to meet so I don't need to make an effort'

How convenient it would be if life didn't involve effort; if we were always head-hunted for jobs rather than having to apply for them; if a law degree and MBA could be implanted in our heads by a neurosurgeon; if good character could be bought at a supermarket. Yet the worthwhile things in life require hard work.

Christians sometimes believe that finding a marriage partner takes no effort because of two factors. First, they know of many people who have met when they were not trying to find a partner, and secondly, they believe that God will provide their partner because that's part of his job.

Our basic theology here is crucially important. If we believe that every event in life is determined by God, right down to what brand of baked beans we buy, then we will not make an effort. We will imbibe a victim mentality, seeing life as something that is happening to us rather than something we have any real influence over. We will become passive and won't bother going to places where we might meet a Christian partner, because if we were going to meet someone God would make it happen anyway. By contrast, look at the biblical heroes of our faith. They certainly sought God's guidance and blessing, but they were also men and women of action who 'laid hold of that for which God has laid hold of me'. They combined heavenly vision and earthly energy. God has placed in my heart the vision of being married. My faith is demonstrated not only in my prayers for a wife, but in my active looking.

Here's another thought to chew on. A scientist on the radio told of how he had three interests as a schoolboy: physics, art and cricket. The last was his greatest passion, but he didn't have the ability to play professionally. Because his school physics laboratory overlooked the Oval cricket ground he was able to combine two of his interests! Years later, as a successful physicist, he returned to the school to preside at a school prize-giving. While wandering around the old corridors he found that the old physics laboratory was now the arts room. On the radio he pondered whether he would now be an artist if the room had had its new function in his day.

The point of telling the tale here is to ask whether

you think it was chance or destiny. Did he have free choice over which career he entered? There is a vital issue here which is reflected in whether we think we have a calling or a destiny. A belief in having a calling urges us actively to participate in fulfilling God's desire for our lives. A belief in destiny makes us think it will happen anyway.

Fantasy number five: 'They will change after I marry them'

You must have heard the joke – it's a regular in wedding sermons – the one in which the bride mutters to herself as she walks down the church, 'Aisle Altar Hymn.' But do husbands, or for that matter wives, change after weddings? As I survey the wreckage of some failed Christian marriages I find that common causes include alcoholism and psychiatric illness. Conditions which were known about before the wedding. Why did their spouses marry them? Again you find that accompanying the couple down the aisle were our old friends 'desperation' and 'falling in love'.

> **True friendships can only flourish between people who regard each other as equals – where there is an opportunity for mutual sharing of strengths and weaknesses.**

Or maybe it was actually genuine Christian love – the committed, caring devotion that is the oxygen of relationships. Such love is so exalted in Scripture that in 1 John it is written that 'God is love'. But true friendships can only flourish between people who regard each other as equals – where there is an opportunity for mutual sharing of strengths and weaknesses. And likewise marriages need interdependency to thrive. Not the one-way dependency that can develop if, for example, your partner is a drug addict.

If you agree with me so far, we may be about to part company, because the most common 'they'll change' delusion cherished by Christians is, 'My partner will accept Jesus after we marry.' Sharing our spirituality is a crucial part of a healthy interdependent relationship. Marriages in which there is a substantial distance in spiritual outlook are not only limited in sharing, but also in the values that bind the parties together. Your partner will not recognise that they are making their marriage vows before God. It is likely to be a lop-sided affair. And tragically, many of these 'unequally yoked' marriages end up with one of the spouses losing their faith or in the marriage failing. I'm writing these sentences after having just been chatting to a Christian woman who is divorced with two young children. She married a non-Christian because there was simply no one else. He ran off with a barmaid. He had different values and different gods. In the following chapters I return to the problem of there not being enough eligible partners to choose from in your church. But let us not make marriage our god.

Fantasy number six: 'I'm called to be single'

You may be thinking, 'Now he really *is* being outrageous. How can he write that people can't be
called to be single?' But I'm not saying that. There
are clear biblical examples of people being called to
be single: the prophet Jeremiah, the eunuchs Jesus
spoke of, as well as the youth of Corinth whom Paul
addressed. Indeed, if only today's church had as
much respect for the single as the writers of the
New Testament did there would not be a need to
write much of this book.

> **Too many Christians regard the fact
> that they have not found a partner to
> date as evidence that God wants them
> to stay single for the rest of their lives.**

What I am questioning is whether *you* have been
called to be single. Too many Christians regard the
fact that they have not found a partner to date as
evidence that God wants them to stay single for the
rest of their lives. Though they have a strong desire
to marry, they are under the impression that God
wants them to be denied this pleasure. This is a
wrong view of God, whose heart is to bless us. He
delights in marriage, and the writers of Scripture are
insistent that it is not a sin to marry. If your desire is
to marry, then I suspect that it is a desire given to you
by God. What people are confusing is the difference
between accepting the reality that for the moment at
least there is no marriage partner in sight, and a

clear, purposeful calling to be single. God has tasks for some people which do not fit well with marriage. Some of these projects may last a lifetime and so call for permanent celibacy. Others may be short term. (Indeed my publishers discussed including a clause in my contract that I should remain single while writing this book!) Whatever the reason for and the length of our calling to singleness, God will give us joy in doing his will.

However, there is a huge difference between this purposeful calling to singleness and the hopefully contented acceptance that for the moment there is no one for me. If we indulge ourselves in the fantasy that God has called us to be single when he has not, then not only will we tend to have a 'why bother?' attitude with the opposite sex, but we'll also have a subconscious anger towards God. Again, this fantasy is an easy one to fall prey to if you have a victim mindset which tells you that God and the world are against you. It springs from a deterministic, fatalistic attitude to life that does not acknowledge the free will God has given you.

There is another group of people who take refuge behind the idea that they have been called to singleness: people who have complicated psychological reasons that are making them avoid relationships with the opposite sex. Perhaps they were hurt in a previous relationship. If you think that you are called to be single, make sure that this is not a mask hiding other issues in your life.

OK, so I will not assume that just because I've fallen

in love with someone this means that we would have a good marriage. Nor will I insist on a potential partner being perfect, or expect them to be parachuted into my life with no effort. And I realise that whoever I marry is the person whom I will have to live with.

But isn't this all too cold and cerebral? Where's the fun and the passion in such calculation – fun and passion that lift relationships from the mundane into the sublime? Where's the scope for the heartfelt conviction that God has brought a couple together? Well, I agree. We do need emotion in relationships. Lots of it! And it is great for a couple to know that they have both submitted their relationship to God and that he is blessing it. But we need thinking as well. Thinking which is like the lighthouse warning us off the rocks. The intellectual shallowness of so much of the church has left our generation lazy about thinking, and it denies that our minds have been made by God.

Take the analogy of a three-legged stool. If a relationship cannot be justified on rational, spiritual and emotional grounds, then it could well disappoint. It needs three sturdy legs of broadly equal length in order to be stable. If our relationship decisions are all passion and spirituality but short on judgement, they will balance precariously. Likewise if they work on cerebral and spiritual levels but lack the passion of the heart, they will ultimately shrivel.

The next chapters look at how we can bring passion, commonsense and spirituality together in seeking a spouse.

SECTION THREE
The Dating Game

11
Who Am I After and Where Can I Meet Them?

Finding someone you want to marry and then winning them over is the most difficult task of your life. Becoming a Christian – the most important decision of your life – is simple by comparison. That the one true God should woo his creation with a faultless love is such an unambiguously wonderful offer that it is ludicrous to refuse. Romance is different. There is a multitude of potential partners – and all with faults.

My burden up to this point in the book has been to encourage you to set your soul free for romance. I have argued for realism about marriage in place of both secular cynicism and starry-eyed idealism. I have urged you to build up your self-esteem so that you should begin to see yourself as the raw material of other people's dreams. And in the last chapter I pleaded with you to spare yourself the ordeal of believing that there is only one person meant for you. That leads to either naive choices or perpetual singleness, because no one can live up to your impossible standards of perfection. Yes, we do want to marry an excellent partner, but if everyone goes around endlessly looking for the best imaginable partners, then we will all be for ever single. And that is precisely what a lot of us are doing. So what should I be looking for and where can I find him or her?

Who?

1. Christian

Let's start with the tough one first. Should you only go out with people who share your faith? There are some real hard-liners on this question who, quoting Paul's injunction against being 'unequally yoked with non-believers', give people who go out with non-Christians a tough time. Many of these purists are the crass, insensitive types who, while ruling out 97 per cent of the population for you, won't lift a finger to help you find a well-matched Christian.

Well, I agree with them. Not with their methods, but with their message. That is because so many have lost their faith by dating non-Christians that this is a crisis for the church, as well as being a defining issue for your and my Christian walk. How can we, who love our God so intimately, contemplate sharing our most intimate human relationship with a non-believer? It is an impossible struggle to daily deepen both our relationship with God and our relationship with a spouse who does not acknowledge God. Something will give. Your partner may give up on you because he or she cannot communicate with you on an issue which is so important to you. Or you will start to withdraw from your faith. If both relationship and faith survive, then both will be impoverished. If you are considering going out with or marrying a non-Christian, ask those in your church who are married to non-believers about the pressures. Ask them about the weekly dilemmas over whether or not to go to a church meeting. Ask them about the daily conflict over how to raise the children.

Think now before it is too late. For when we fall in love with a non-Christian we will start to lower our standards regarding pre-marital sex, and then we will find ourselves being sucked away from our faith like a feather before a vacuum cleaner. The passion for our new-found love, the guilt we feel about our pre-marital sex – these do not make it easy to sit comfortably in church. You simply cannot compartmentalise your life.

I am very aware that God does often step into these situations and marvellously bring unbelievers to a real and lasting faith. I have seen this in my own family. But we should not presume upon this grace. And rather than looking inwardly on our own longing for intimacy, we should look at the impact of our actions on other single Christians. If I start a relationship with a non-believer, I will be adding to the pressures on the other single men and women in my church already tempted to do the same.

If going out with a non-Christian is a sin, Scripture teaches us that 'we who are spiritual' should gently try to restore those who are rebelling in this way. Instead, we are often heavy-handed in our 'advice' and only further alienate those who are already beginning to slip away. Genuine compassion involves entering into the sufferings of those who are in turmoil. We need to understand their anguish and be with them as they struggle with their feelings of temptation and guilt and the spiritual need to surrender the only human tenderness they may have known in years. The following are two real examples.

Janet started seeing Anthony towards the end of her second year at university. Her friends remember her zeal for her faith, how she was committed to working overseas as a missionary after university. Anthony and she were an excellent match. There was a real rapport between them, fed by a common passion for art and literature. He didn't share her faith, but there again he wasn't antagonistic, and in going out he put no pressure on her whatsoever to stop going to church or to get involved sexually. If ever going out with a non-Christian appeared to be low risk, then this was it. But they fell in love with each other and there was less room for God. The more passionately Janet felt for Anthony, the more natural it was to get physical. They started living together and the guilt she felt made her feel awkward with the Christian friends she had built up over the years. Now a year after university she and he are both working overseas and very much in love. But her faith which once burned so brightly is nowhere. It happened so gradually that she may not have been very aware of it happening, but she has travelled a huge distance spiritually.

Carol started seeing Peter at the same university. She was a young Christian recently come alive in her faith. He may not have been particularly good-looking, but he still seemed a good catch. They started seeing each other and Carol came under a lot of flak from her Christian friends for dating a non-believer. Yet through the grace of God and Peter's free will, he came to faith. Seventeen years on he remains steadfast in his faith, committed to evangelism and to his wife of the past fifteen years. With a steady marriage, a strong faith and two fine young sons, Carol and Peter represent the life aspired to by many singles who are hungry for love. But why Carol was fortunate enough for her partner to become a Christian and Janet wasn't, I cannot explain.

For those older or isolated Christians who yearn for marriage but see no suitable Christians nearby, the temptation is to adopt a 'convert your own' strategy. But this is gambling eternity for a man, the stake being the most important thing you have – your faith. You *may* end up with a Christian spouse, but far too many lose on this gamble.

Whether we are friends, pastors or church leaders we have to show thoughtful care towards those being tempted by mixed relationships. We have to work out all the reasons why they and others are being drawn into these romances, as well as how best to help them out of wrong relationships and into right ones. My primary motivation in writing this book is that our God-given desire for relationship should no longer be a source of weakness for the kingdom of God, but one of its strengths. We lose so many through dating non-Christians that this issue is a crisis for the church.

2. *Compatibility*

So what else is on your checklist at the moment? Go on, lie to me and say that good looks aren't an issue for you! Let me be honest with you and tell you what's on my checklist. She has to be Oxbridge educated, have been a Christian for roughly as long as I have, a well-balanced personality, younger than I am, quite pretty, under 5'8" tall, live reasonably close to London and like garlic (the last point is optional). Now tell me why I'm not married! Am I being reasonable? OK, I'm not, but are you? You too have a list. You too have a salami-slicing approach to suitable people that rules out most of humanity, let alone Christendom. On the rare occasion that we meet a creature matching our criteria we are such gibbering wrecks that they don't look twice at us!

So what should we do? Throw out our checklists? Well no, because as with most of the ways we approach the dating scene, there is an element of wisdom in them. But we should consider holding onto our 'lists' a little less tightly. If we are not dating many people, it is either because we are not coming across enough suitable people (read on!), or we are being too restrictive about who we are meeting.

As well as increasing the number of places where we meet Christians, we could do well to set ourselves targets about how many people we date. If you do not have at least one one-to-one meeting with a

different 'eligible' every month, then I would con-
tend that you are probably being too narrow. You are
putting iron walls around you that lock out the very
thing you want.

In addition to challenging ourselves over how
tightly we have drawn our criteria, we also need to
look very carefully at each individual criterion to see
how important it is. For when we are sixty-five and
looking back at our five years of marriage (the way
we're going I can't see us getting hitched before
sixty!), what will be important? I don't think looks
will rank very highly, although that is the one thing
we all seem to make a god out of in dating.

Here's my evidence. An NOP poll in *The Guardian*
newspaper in February 1997 asked couples who had
been married for ten or more years what they liked
most about their partner. The most popular answer,
mentioned by 18 per cent, was that they were 'caring
and thoughtful'. Some 17 per cent said 'everything'
(isn't that lovely!), 10 per cent mentioned their
spouse's personality and only 1 per cent said the
thing liked most was their partner's looks. The
biggest surprise of all to me was that sex also only
scored (sorry!) 1 per cent. Now all of the 794 couples
mentioned have been married for at least ten years.
We singles all want marriages which will last, so
wouldn't it be sensible for us to rearrange our priorities when it comes to who we chase in the dating
game?

We singles all want marriages which will last, so wouldn't it be sensible for us to rearrange our priorities when it comes to who we chase in the dating game?

3. *Conversation*

Now isn't that quaint – the notion that a couple will look back at their marriage and reflect on how much they liked talking to each other? Yet good talk is not only one of the most enjoyable parts of marriage and the pleasure that takes up more time than any other, it will also save your marriage. Unless the two of you are utterly at liberty in talking with each other, then you will be poor at diffusing the problems building up. Conversation is the safety valve. Time after time divorce counsellors hear wives and husbands saying that their spouse was hopeless at talking. If, therefore, you want a marriage that will last years and years, look for people with whom you can talk for hours and hours without getting bored. And someone who is committed to communicating with you.

4. *Character*

You are looking for someone who is going to commit the rest of his or her life to living with you – despite your snoring, your phobia about housework and your inability to use a watch. Now they are going to need some staying power to put up with decades of you! It is no use marrying the prettiest girl in the choir or the handsomest hunk in the church if they haven't got character. Girls, you need a man who will get up for the third time that night to settle your crying child. Men, you need a woman who will be just as committed to you if you are fired from your high flying City job and forced to sign on the dole. So many of the things we major on at the dating stage will look completely ephemeral a few years into marriage.

Character gives substance to all the wedding vows your spouse makes to you.

Look at it another way. Talk is cheap. When we're dating, the words 'I love you' can often be no more than part of the male sales patter known as charm. Even when there is sincerity and thought behind them, they can be meaningless unless the person speaking has the character that will back up words with action when it is not personally convenient. The evidence of character is not the sweet nothings you whisper to each other, but the way she reacts when your car has broken down in the pouring rain on the way to the theatre. Or the way he reacts when you've reversed your car into the back of his. Only time and the insights of those who know your potential spouse can show whether they have character.

Character gives substance to all the wedding vows your spouse makes to you. I could write you a cheque for £1 million, but my bank manager will not honour it. Your partner's character is their ability to honour their promises to you. Everything on my checklist is meaningless unless she has character. In marriage it is the pearl of great price.

5. Chemistry

This is the wild card. Some see 'chemistry' as a euphemism for falling in love. Others as another name for sexual attraction. Or is it what might be described as the way some couples 'click'? Certainly there are people we immediately get on with. When on first meeting we feel that we have known each other for years, it is an intuitive response to us having years of similar experiences behind us, as well as similar expectations of the years to come. We have a harmony of heritage and vision. When this ties in with a subtle sense of sexual rapport and a confidence that we both have the emotional resources to support each other, then the chemistry is occurring on several levels. It is an unspoken acknowledgement of mutual attraction; that physically, emotionally and intellectually the two of us communicate. It is this ability to communicate on all levels which is the very essence of a successful relationship.

I guess I should be a preacher. Five points on what to look for in the ideal partner and they all began with the same letter!

Before we move on to where we can find suitable candidates for the job of spouse, there is another reason why our generation of 'wannabe' marrieds are failing to walk down the aisle. Expectations. Let me illustrate this.

A friend of a friend is a Christian from Sri Lanka. She flew back to Colombo to meet the son of one of her parents' friends whom it was thought might be suitable. He had flown from his home in Singapore to meet her. After just two meetings they decided to get married, and a few years on the marriage continues to go well. Now the point here is not about the pros and cons of arranged marriages. It is the issue of expectations. This couple regarded each other as reasonably matched. They took the risk of marriage because they didn't expect a perfect match, but a good match. Their expectations of marriage were more modest than ours, but their commitment to make it work very high. The result is happiness. (This jet-setting relationship is very different from the one I mentioned in Chapter 5 where an Australian was flying to London to meet a boyfriend. While that appeared to be a romance designed to avoid having to make any hard decision about commitment, in this Asian example the couple are very realistic both in terms of expectations of marriage and their willingness to make a decision to marry.)

Our modern Western expectations are utterly different. We look for near on 100 per cent perfection in the compatibility stakes before we take the immense risk of entering an irrevocable commitment. While this has a veneer of commonsense, the reality is that we will never be happily married. First, because no one will come up to our standard of suitability, and secondly, because even if we did find the perfect candidate, our sky-high view of marriage would mean that at very best we would be merely satisfied. We try to take the risk out of marriage by looking for someone perfect. This is so secular, for faith is about taking risks before God.

We who seek 100 per cent so often end up with 0 per cent – no marriage. Then as the years roll by, in our desperation we will get hitched to Mr or Miss 40 per cent. If we aimed at, say, 80 per cent we might actually find people who exist and marry one of them. This is no mere theory. Too many of my friends who turned down good opportunities in the past have, now that the years pass by, started to date non-Christians or marry divorcees.

We try to take the risk out of marriage by looking for someone perfect. This is so secular, for faith is about taking risks before God.

Looks and loot

So maybe you strongly agree with me: 'Yes, of course we should beware of being trapped by absurdly high expectations.' But I know what you and I will be doing at church on Sunday evening. Searching out the fairest of the fair. Dismissing in split seconds those who don't measure up to the looks we're searching for. We'll be closing down conversations with 'potentials', instantly crossing them off the list, because of some perceived failing in terms of education or income. You do it and I do it. And everyone else is doing it. The result is that making new friends on the Christian scene is an uphill struggle. Either we've already dismissed them as partner material or they've dismissed us. We need to work out our theology of romance (how God would have us date) and then plead with God daily to renew our minds so that the old ways of thinking which have become so ingrained give way to the freedom of following God's paths for our romantic lives.

Where are they hiding?

1. Other churches

Surely not. How could I suggest you do something as deeply unspiritual as touring around neighbouring churches checking out the talent? Well, tell yourself you are being ecumenical, building bridges between local congregations. That's much more spiritual-sounding. If you are an Anglican and you suspect that there may be some rather nice members of the opposite sex at the local Baptist church, then become a Baptist for a day. In an ideal world the ministers of the two churches would be getting their singles together. If they're not, be helpful and create your own unofficial links. There is nothing theologically dubious in wanting to get married, but it is unspiritual to worry about it. So stop the paralysis by analysis and get out there. My loyalty to my local church is not compromised by the occasional foray into other parts of the kingdom of God.

There is nothing theologically dubious in wanting to get married, but it is unspiritual to worry about it.

---

2. Conferences and courses

Meet new people at church and it tends to be a case of snatching a few words over a cup of dodgy coffee after the service. Christian conferences and courses by comparison offer the opportunity to hold proper conversations. There are a whole load of these, ranging from one-day prayer meetings, to six months with YWAM. I thoroughly commend them, not only because they offer a great way to meet 'someone special', but you just might find that God takes advantage of the course to do a deep work in your life!

3. Church offices

Joining the staff of, say, the local diocesan office or a Christian charity is an excellent way of meeting a mate. Not only are you often working with many other single Christians who are enthusiastic about their faith, but most of the people passing through the office will also fit into this category. This is a superb way not only to come across new people, but also to see them under the pressures of everyday life. The only drawback with this approach is whether you can afford the cut in pay. But there again, can you afford not to?

4. Christian holidays

I have never been on an Oak Hall holiday, and I am still single. Are the two facts connected? The reputation for romance of some of the Christian package holidays is spectacular. (I met the lady I was once engaged to on a Mastersun holiday in Italy!) While spending a week or two with Christians in a relaxed environment does give the opportunity to learn a lot about someone, the approach also has its drawbacks. First, you are not seeing your romantic interest in their real habitat. Secondly, they may live hundreds of miles away from you.

By the way, please don't do what one girl did on a Christian holiday in Turkey. She got off the plane, onto the coach, surveyed the 'available' Christian men and went into a depressed sulk for the whole week. Go on holiday first for a holiday. Meeting someone is a delightful bonus.

5. Innovative dating

How about holding a buffet party to which you invite half-a-dozen male and female friends on the understanding that each of them will bring a couple of interesting people of their own sex whom nobody else will know? They won't want to bring 'lemons' along and everyone has an incentive to make the evening work.

Or take the example of Jo who is at university in Bristol. Every Sunday after church she invites men she likes for lunch. Sometimes it's just one. Often it's a group. But either way she's a good cook, so they don't say 'no'! After lunch she and her target(s) will typically go for a walk. Jo's approach has two main advantages. First, being invited to Sunday lunch is hardly a high pressure date. And secondly, eating and walking give a couple a great opportunity to talk and get to know each other – much more so than, for example, going to the cinema.

6. Networking

This is the job-hunting approach. Decide what you want and systematically put out the word through anyone you know who might know someone suitable. Do so boldly, without a hint of embarrassment. Be outrageous – cold-call church leaders you've never even met and ask if they know anyone who might be suitable for you. Suggest that you are doing them a favour by meeting some of their singles, and don't take 'no' for an answer. Persist until, like the 'unjust judge' Jesus speaks of, they decide that the only way to get rid of you is to help.

This type of approach is exactly what people who get jobs in journalism do. They don't get discouraged by the odds against them, or by the editors who try to fob them off. Instead they demonstrate the depth of their determination until the people with influence and connections are willing at least to see them. Be a guerrilla, using any method, however unorthodox, because you know that your cause is righteous.

7. Dating agencies

In theory Christian dating agencies provide a very powerful tool for matching people. The breakdown of community life has removed so many of the social networks that used to facilitate the first meetings of many couples. A generation ago Mrs Jones would have told her friend, Mr Brown, that somebody had moved into the town who might be suitable for his daughter. Today dating agencies should fill that gap, linking together suitable people from small church communities around the country.

And dating agencies can provide superior matches to other methods. 'Great Expectations', the biggest dating agency in the USA, has 144,000 members. It boasts a divorce rate among its clients who met through the agency of only 5 per cent. Now this figure is remarkably low bearing in mind that half of all marriages in the USA end in divorce. The statistics appear to be reliable and what I suspect is going on is that members are tending only to date people with whom they are highly compatible. The size of the agency means that there are lots of such matches available and after a fair few dates, many find someone with whom there is very strong chemistry as well as compatibility. If such a couple decide to commit themselves to each other in marriage, there is an infinitely better chance of the relationship working out than there is in the usual approach of dating people we fancy at parties.

American dating agencies thrive on the open-minded, go-for-it mentality found in the 'Land of Opportunity'. We Brits are much more conservative. We see dating agencies as an admission of failure rather than an additional opportunity for meeting people. If our parents didn't use them, then why should we? It's only when our friends have filled in the application form for us and sent it off that we can be frog-marched towards this opportunity.

Unfortunately for British Christians the prejudice becomes self-fulfilling. Britain's cottage industry of Christian dating agencies is awash with the 'hard-to-place'. Any 'highly eligibles' who do join find themselves confronted with Leering Larry, the social inadequate, or Desperate Donna, who on the first date tells you about her desire to have four children. Most agencies appear to have only a few hundred members and are therefore unable to offer even vaguely compatible matches in terms of age, location, education and height. Some of my up-market friends at church even pay hundreds of pounds for the professionalism of secular agencies, even though very few of these agencies' members will be Christians.

I hope that what I have written will be of use, or at least stir your imagination as to the endless possible places where great Christian partners hang out.

12
How to Say 'Hello'

The Christian dating scene resembles a camel with
two humps. One hump gets on with it. They'll ask
out or say 'yes' to anyone they fancy without worrying about what other people think. They come across
as secure in themselves and confident about their
attractiveness to the opposite sex. Life for them
seems to be one long invitation. And at parties
they go to it's not a question of whether they'll
meet anyone, but who they'll go out with.

The other hump holds pity parties. Except no one
comes. They haven't been out with anyone for ages
and they get locked into a downward spiral as falling
confidence makes them less willing to take any risks
with the opposite sex. The longer they stay out of
circulation, the more unsure of themselves with the
opposite sex they become – something that potential
partners pick up on. Take two of my mates.

I share a flat with Paul, an amiable rogue in his
thirties who's been a Christian longer than most.
This week he's dating five women. He rolled in last
night from a blind date with an upper-crust woman
he had first spoken to when she phoned his office
number by mistake! Paul liked the sound of her voice

and rather than simply hang up after saying 'wrong number', he had the enterprise to keep her talking for twenty minutes. They exchanged phone numbers and after talking several more times on the phone she agreed to meet him. What surprised me was that this woman – met through chance – turned out to be an active churchgoer. Now, after the date, Paul reckons that the two of them aren't that suited, but what his action does is give an insight into how much richer a social life the risk-takers have.

Then there's another chap, whom I will call Simon. Not an excessively confident person to start with, he has over the past few months asked two women out for dates after getting the impression that his interest was reciprocated. On both occasions he's been turned down – the first woman may have simply been flirting; the second, while initially interested, had her attention diverted when a better offer came along. But whatever the rights or wrongs of it, for Simon it is a case of twice bitten thrice shy. He is now extremely hesitant about asking anyone out. It could be quite a long time before he next makes a move, and given what an ordeal it has been for him, he's not likely to come across as hugely confident. After all, there's only so much rejection a fellow can take! So the confident become more confident and the unsure become even more unsure.

Now by dint of the number of Christian women who complain that they never get asked out, I reckon that there are loads more Simons than there are Pauls. So what are we to do about the often depressingly static Christian dating scene?

Calling all who represent the second hump of our camel, here are a few ideas to help you shift to that front hump!

Have fun

Now here's a radical thought. Dating should be fun, not a time-consuming ordeal that we spend every other waking moment worrying about. Not a fraught game of poker in which no one dares to reveal their hand. Not a process that will determine whether you will have a sex life or spend all your days alone. No, dating should be a laugh, getting to know members of the opposite sex. It should be hilarious – doing whacky things, swapping crazy stories and living life to the full.

Dating should be fun, not a time-consuming ordeal that we spend every other waking moment worrying about.

To make sure that we are speaking the same language when it comes to dealing with requests for dates, we desperately need to agree on some ground rules. And I would suggest that we should start with a dating scene where a date is simply a social meeting without any expectations, exclusivity or snogging rights implied. When you ask someone out, or agree to a date, you are merely planning to have some holy fun together for a few hours. It is not a declaration that you think they are the one meant for you. That interpretation is enough to put anyone off because it's tantamount to a guy saying to a girl he hardly knows, 'I want to spend half of my life snoring next to you in bed, and the rest of the time irritating you with my other bad habits.'

The more we date people in a relaxed manner, the more friendships we will develop with the opposite sex, out of which romances can grow. Far too much of the Christian scene is dominated by people trying to assess each other's suitability for marriage at a thousand yards. Just as you can't read a book at that distance so we need to get to meet each other face to face in order to understand what makes each other tick.

By definition, if you and your potential date have never been out with each other, you don't know each other, even if you have spent lots of time in a group. So asking for or agreeing to a date does not have to be a huge decision. We are simply seeing if there is potential for friendship. Only if a friendship is firmly established do we really need to think about 'going out' in an exclusive fashion.

When we decide not to ask someone out or we decline to go out with someone, it should be on the basis that we think the compatibility is so limited that there is no chance of even a friendship developing, let alone a romance. Let us not judge people against the 'ideal spouse' yardstick until we have got to know them. So long as a request for a date or the acceptance of a date is seen as strongly implying an interest in marriage, then the Christian dating scene will remain dysfunctional. We have to chill out.

Only when individuals have met lots of people through dating are they in a position to know what is truly important for them in the opposite sex, otherwise they have no comparison. And if a couple who have become friends through dating decide to go out – to make their relationship exclusive – then each of them is dealing with a known quantity.

Of course sometimes things move very quickly, and an intense relationship is underway before the underlying friendship has developed. I've been there. And sometimes it works. But generally getting serious with someone you hardly know is not ideal. I would suggest that a relaxed approach to dating, getting to know a lot of different people slowly, should be the norm. Now to my second radical idea!

Ask the blokes out

Now let's get this straight. This is advice to the sisters! After being deeply correct thoughout this book I don't want to upset the evangelical thought police at this late stage. Having sorted that out, I can immediately hear the women chorus, 'But we're good Christian girls who would never do anything as tacky as ask men out.'

Call me insensitive, but I think that is a load of tosh. First, it is *not* a sign of immorality to ask a man out. It does not imply that you are either 'easy' or 'desperate'. Rather it signals that you are a woman of determination who knows what she wants and isn't prepared to sit around passively for the next few decades waiting for it to happen. Nor is pursuing men unbiblical – look at that marvellous woman of integrity, Ruth. Having been given the idea by

Naomi, it is Ruth who makes the move on Boaz. Not only does she get her man, but Boaz makes it clear that he does not think any the less of her for being forward. Rather he assures her: 'All my fellow towns-men know that you are a woman of noble character.' My only criticism of Ruth is that I think uncovering Boaz's feet was a mean trick to play!

There's more. In chapter 3 of Song of Songs our friend the 'rose of Sharon' does not sit at home moping about her beloved not being anywhere in sight. No, she gets up in the middle of the night and wanders around the city until she finds him. What went on next is best reserved for after wedding vows are exchanged, but the Bible is again speaking approvingly of a woman actively looking for a man. This picture of women taking the initiative is painted against the backdrop of a highly patriarchal society thousands of years ago, so what excuse is there for modern Christian women living in an increasingly egalitarian society to sit around like wallflowers?

One reason, sisters, is that your thinking is still dominated by the habits of a male-dominated society in which men did all the choosing. The other, more powerful reason, is fear of rejection. You, like the lads, simply don't like to risk getting turned down. But which is worse? Sitting around whinging as the man of your dreams, and possibly marriage itself, passes you by? Or being strong and courageous? Since we fellas know all too well the agonies of asking people out, maybe you just might find us remarkably sympathetic if you ask us out.

Courage and clarity

I find our Christian dating scene so exasperating. The sheer stupidity of us all. Take a friend of mine, who strongly suspected that a man she liked was also keen on her. But neither had the guts to say so. Neither was willing to become vulnerable to rejection by someone they had grown fond of. They both attended the same church and I guess both feared that word would get around if either of them approached the other. Now, a few months on, she has given up on him, and she's not bothering to talk to him. It's so sad. And so typical.

I have a wonderful photograph of my first serious romance. She's clutching a bunch of pink carnations given by yours truly and she is beaming. I had just asked her out and all over her face is written 'He likes me!' Unfortunately, at that very moment, I was trudging back to my student digs thinking, 'She doesn't like me. Oh well . . . at least I asked.' Alas, her response to my statement, 'I would like to spend more time with you,' had been, 'But, Ian, you've got exams this term.' What she thought was an expression of concern I took as a polite turn-down. I graduated and forgot about her. She wondered why I had never followed up on my apparent initial interest. Then six months later a letter arrived on my door mat with unfamiliar handwriting. She had heard through a mutual friend that I had indeed cared for her and sent a letter wondering, if there was no one else . . . was it now too late? It wasn't! We spent a happy year dating.

> **Only God knows how many brilliant romances have passed us by because we could not muster the courage to make ourselves clear.**

If it hadn't been for her courage we would not have dated. Whether the initial misunderstanding was down to me or her it matters not. The point is that when someone like you or me is nervously expressing interest in a member of the opposite sex, the words being sputtered out may not be clear. And even if they aren't opaque the listener can still get the wrong impression. Only God knows how many brilliant romances have passed us by because we could not muster the courage to make ourselves clear.

Imagine the following scenario:

He says: I wonder whether you are free on Tuesday?
He's thinking: There, I've said it at last . . . I've asked her if she will be my girlfriend.
She's hearing: Is Tuesday a convenient day?
She says: I'm sorry, I'm tied up then.
She means: There are plenty of other days when I am free.
He thinks: She's not interested.

If you are going to summon up the courage to ask someone out, you must be fair to yourself and be utterly clear about your intentions to the other party, for you are making yourself vulnerable – showing your heart's desire and risking rejection.

Gossip

Going out with someone is more risk-laden when you know them well, and both of you are concerned about your relationship becoming the talk of the congregation. In my church a number of people have moved to a neighbouring congregation after splitting up with someone in the church. I switched home groups after stopping going out with one girl. There is so much less pressure if you go out with someone who isn't known to your group of friends — someone who isn't already a key part of your social life. But this leads to the appalling situation where the people we know well and really like are the people we *don't* ask out. When there is too much at stake in terms of the existing friendship, we only date strangers. This should not be.

For his eyes only – a private letter to men

Dear Brother,

Where are we going wrong? Why aren't we having more success? I've been asking around some girls and they've been giving a few helpful hints about where we're blundering.

The first thing they say is that we're obsessed with looks and only ask out the prettiest girls. Well, that's completely untrue because I know a friend of a friend who, about ten years ago, asked out a really quite plain-looking woman. But guys, maybe they do have a point. While it's nice to have a doll on your arm who makes your mates jealous, I guess we should be looking for a wife, not a status symbol, and for that we need someone who is emotionally together and interesting. Pretty girls who qualify in those areas are in short supply. In any case, who wants a wife whom other men will still be chasing after you've put a ring on her finger? I'm not denying the importance of finding your wife sexually attractive, but by aiming at the supermodel level we're not only reducing our chances of going out with anyone, but we're probably missing out on a lot better wife material sitting next to us at church. And she is probably dying for us guys to ask her out. So don't bother with the very pretty ones – if they are interested in us I'm afraid they're going to have to ask us out.

Moving on from *who* we're after to *what* we're after. Women find it quite crazy how we guys will risk a lifetime of sexual pleasure with them for the sake of a quick grope. We'll push our luck, venture into uninvited body space and then wonder why they dump us. Guys, when we're dating we're under inspection. Pushy men come across to women as careless about their sexual integrity and probably less likely to qualify on the faithful husband stakes.

Women also have queries about the way we ask them out. Most of them are merely acquaintances when we first ask them out and we're expecting them to become star-struck lovers. It's a big step. Why not make it very clear that what we're after first of all is moving from being acquaintances to friends? This is not only a matter of vocabulary, but also of the type of date we're asking them out on. Some girls would love to be invited straight away to the ballet. Others

who may well want to get to know you better might
be much happier with the halfway house of a meal in
a restaurant, or something as low key as a walk in
the park. Instant relationships rarely work, so let's
not frighten her off, but raise the tempo gradually.
Perhaps the ideal is the friendship that gradually
drifts into being a romance without any tense
moments of 'asking out'. The relationships which
break up with the vacuous words, 'Let's be friends,'
would have had a much better chance if they had
started off as friendships.

Towards this end try and casually date loads of
women. Then if any of them say that they're washing
their hair, it does not come as such a blow to your
persona. Simply put it down to them having slightly
misjudged the type of date you were requesting. And
don't worry about the risk that some women will get
the wrong idea and think that you are considering
marriage when you've just asked them out for a date.
If they do that's their responsibility. Your responsibility is merely to make yourself clear. Their feelings
are their problem. In any case, as word spreads that
you are a 'relaxed' dater and that you 'behave', not
only will more women be happy to go out with you,
but they'll also have the right idea.

When you are trying to up the ante, do so subtly.
Don't kiss her out of the blue, rather play to her
feminine instincts. I am told that small romantic
gifts, like a tiny box of chocolates or some trinket
jewellery, can start to alter perceptions. It doesn't
matter if the gift is cheap, as long as it displays
thoughtfulness. At the right time, poetry can be a

complete winner – something to do with us men 'articulating our inner emotions' that women find attractive. Simply being a nice, caring bloke is not enough. Women want a man who makes them feel wanted. And if you can't get the romantic stuff together when you are courting, then you are going to make a lousy husband. If you demonstrate that you are romantic, attentive and have learned the skills of appropriate flattery, then she feels valued.

Women also tell me that they want a man with an air of 'take charge sophistication'. A relaxed confidence rather than a forced impression of it. Deepseated security is a powerful aphrodisiac. It's a gift that you have but you may not be using. So start to exercise more initiative and your confidence will grow – just like muscles in a gym.

Finally, never let an opportunity to get to know a nice Christian woman pass you by. I kick myself that when I was chatting to a girl at church recently I did not ask for her telephone number. We were both enjoying talking to each other and she might well have been agreeable to an 'appropriate' date, but because I lacked the courage we may never meet again. We have to seize every moment. In a Christian culture where so many guys talk a lot about women but don't talk *to* them, the way is open for you and me to take advantage of their inadequacy.

Yours sincerely,

Ian

I now welcome back my female readers who didn't read the last section. Men can skip the next section.

For her eyes only – a letter to my female readers

Dear Sister,

Are you a Sinbad (Single Income No Boyfriend And Desperate)? Well here are a few insights about how that confusing place, the male mind, works.

To start with many Christian women say that men don't ask them out. That's not true, it's just that (a) we spend most of our time asking out that gorgeous girl who sits at the front of the church, (b) you don't count the men who do ask you out because you don't like them or, worst of all, (c) decent men are asking you out but you don't realise it.

What can we do about this distressing state of affairs? Well, let's start with the superficial. Looks are a very cruel business. It's about women, as well as men, dismissing a member of the opposite sex on the basis of a glance. It is utterly unfair on those whose looks are well below average, and perversely unfair on the very beautiful, as they get so inundated with the charm merchants that the best blokes don't bother.

You have the choice of either totally accepting this worldly ideology and spending huge amounts of time and money on making yourself as superficially appealing as possible. Or you can reject it completely, dress in sackcloth and ashes and say that men have got to accept you for what you are on the inside. Why not take a balanced view instead? Just as there are men who could make more effort in losing some weight and taking a little more care with their appearance, there are also women who don't try.

Turning to the men you turn down. Do you tell them why you don't want to go out with them? Is it a case of who they are or how they asked? If it's a case of who they are, then it would be a good discipline for both of you to say why. If it's because you are a duchess and he is a dustman give this as the reason. It forces you both to think about the real issues involved. The purpose is not to change your mind but for both of you to clarify what you really are after in life. If it's his age, his looks, his height, his obsession with Country and Western music or his bad breath, it helps both to know!

If potentially you like him, but his manner of asking is inappropriate, then make a counter-offer rather than rejecting him outright. Respond to his offer of a candlelit supper with the suggestion of lunch; the weekend in Paris with a walk in the country. If you are not sure about him and want to think about it, play for time. Ask him to give you a phone call. We need to have the cunning of diplomats when we are dealing with romance. Instead of simply saying 'no' to a chap, take the opportunity of his courage in asking you out to make it a constructive learning experience for you both.

Another thing. Please don't assume that he will understand the subtexts of what you say. Men communicate in words, not nuances. It's just the way we've been trained. So if, for example, it's only one week since you split up with the love of your life and not the ideal time to start another relationship, then be clear that in a few months' time your response might be different. Otherwise he'll assume it's him you don't like.

The issue of indirect communication brings us to the subject of body language. I'm sorry to be so blunt, but some of you girls are very naive. Take negative body language first. Women who complain that there are no men in their lives should get themselves videoed. The bristling look, the frown, the distracted glance. None of these makes men want to take the risk of wandering up to you to talk. Nor does the armadillo group behaviour in which a number of women start chatting to each other in a circle, shoulder to shoulder, with their backs to the rest of mankind. We would love to talk to you, but we can see that we're not welcome. Your defence mechanism comes across to us as dismissive arrogance.

Then there are the false positives. Take the gormless woman who put her hand on my knee but didn't want to go out. Or the girl who invited a friend of mine round to her flat after midnight, sat down on the sofa with him and then was surprised when he tried to kiss her.

The subject of such physical signals is important because so many successful relationships do start with a kiss. In the secular world the vast majority of relationships start not with a clinical verbal request but a snog! So if a man tries to kiss you and you are not interested, don't be surprised. Just make it clear you are not interested — there's no need to tell your friends that you regard him as a sex attacker. However, if he doesn't understand the word 'no' then he does need a warning sticker on him, and a talking to from the pastor.

It is the concern about men who don't know when to stop – of sexual assault – that leads some women to treat all men with extreme caution. While some of you girls defiantly walk home through inner-city London after midnight ('I'm not going to give in to fear'), others of you are so nervous that you effectively lock men entirely out of your life. If you are fearful, try to suggest alternative venues for dates where you can meet and feel safe.

For men it is not the fear of violence that is inhibiting the dating process, but the fear of ridicule. Say, for example, that I asked you out and you turned me down. (Hard to believe it, but some women have turned me down!) Now could you resist telling your girlfriends about my request? You see, the fear we guys have is that if all your girlfriends know about us being turned down by you then they, in the future, will not want to be seen going out with your reject! If you have a reputation for being a bit of a gossip, then we will not ask you out because it ruins our chances with other women. Can you see why if Christian women do gossip Christian men don't ask them out? If you replicate this fear around a tight-knit church community, you'll see how gossip is like pouring superglue into the engine of romance. Careless talk costs relationships.

Here's another bit of male psychology. Women playing hard to get does not make men go wild. It simply bores them. Few men will fall for the tactic of being kept like a puppy on a string by a woman who for ever portrays herself as being busy, needing to cut short phone-calls and dates. We will either assume that you are genuinely not interested – and forget about you – or take the tactic as a symptom of an immature mind that isn't worth getting to know. If you are interested, show it.

Yours sincerely,

Ian

Welcome back to both sets of readers. I have every confidence that no one has read both letters! Before I press on, I must tell you the tale of Ken, the grandfather of a friend of mine. He's seventy-six years old and was widowed three years ago after fifty years of marriage to the woman he first met when he was fourteen. He is now looking for a new woman in his life. His problem, like ours, is that he just can't read the signals! When down at the British Legion club he meets someone new, he's not sure how to work out if she is interested in him. The old progression of growing commitment – taking a friend to the pictures, then to dances, then to each other's parents – has disappeared. He, like us, spends a great deal of time talking about relationships, because he's so frustrated by the process.

Hold tight . . .

. . . for this book has just become interactive. Before you read any more, get out a pencil and paper and write down the names of five people you would like to date. If you can't think of five people, then you

really need to get the circulation of your social life
moving a little faster. It's no good just rereading the
last chapter on where to find them, you also need to
put it into practice. For those of you with a list of
five (or more!), I have a question. What is your
strategy for approaching each of them? You mean
you have no plan? You are telling me that you haven't
even approached any of them; that they don't know
you like them?

This business of romance should be treated like a
business. Indeed, this life is so short that finding a
marriage partner to build a family with is much
more important than any business. So it is vital
that we not only devise a business plan (or should
it be a battle plan?), but we rigorously follow it
through.

Just as nobody gets a job without talking to the
manager, so none of us gets dates without talking to
those we want to date. For each of our five prospects
let us draw up a list of events we will invite them to,
and then systematically start acting on our plan.

Just as in business or in war, unexpected setbacks
will occur. You'll find out that he's just started going
out with someone else or she's decided to emigrate
(because none of the men in her church ever
expressed any interest in her). But just as there are
setbacks, so there are new opportunities. In chasing
Fred you find that he has an even more interesting
brother called John. In pursuing Jacqui you find that
she has a delightful friend called Janet. Note that
these are possibilities that only emerged because you
started to implement your plan. Dreaming is not

enough. Thinking is not enough. You have to take action. The alternative is numbing.

Dreaming is not enough. Thinking is not enough. You have to take action.

Fixations

We become like Alan. About to go on a YWAM course in Canada, he's convinced that God has told him that he is going to marry a nurse whose name begins with 'M'. So when on the course he meets a nurse called Mary it's obviously meant from above. Mary is not convinced, but Alan is unmoved in his conviction. Ten years later Mary gets engaged . . . to someone else. Alan phones the fiancé and tells him that the marriage is not the will of God. But the fiancé and Mary disagree and get married. Result? A crisis of faith for Alan and ten wasted years of delusion.

There's a little bit of Alan in each of us. Look at the people we have admired from afar without doing anything about it. Like Alan, you and I convince ourselves that we're serious about finding a partner, but often we're operating marriage avoidance strategies. The proof of it is that we spend vast amounts of time thinking about relationships and little or no time doing anything practical about making them happen. Doing can of course be overdone, but I think most of us are a long, long way off being charged with harassment!

Epilogue
Where Do We Go From Here?

I've painted a picture of a poorly functioning Christian dating scene in which large numbers of eligible and compatible men and women simply are not meeting. They may even be going to churches just a few miles away from each other, but with so little social interaction between churches it's just pot-luck whether they will come across each other. Even if they do meet, they've still got to break through their reserved British culture and private uncertainties before relationships can develop.

As individual Christians there is so much we can do to break out of this debilitating scene. If we challenge our own fears, think imaginatively about where we can meet the type of person we're after, and then take the initiative ourselves, we can transform our chances of making a good match this side of the grave.

But beyond our own personal hopes and dreams there are bigger fish to fry. The next millennium is almost upon us and any church which wants to succeed in it has to see that single people are making up an ever growing part of congregations and society as a whole. This is a group which is not just growing

in numbers – already more than a third of society –
but it is one which feels increasingly unhappy within
church. For involuntary singleness among Christians
causes so much heartache, so many defections and
takes up so much pastoral time. We must urgently re-
examine the obstacles to the creation of Christian
marriages.

First and foremost, our theology of romance – that
is our view of how God would have us meet and
match – needs to be radically reassessed. As long as
vast numbers of Christians are taught simply to wait
for God to provide Mr or Miss Right for them, the
longer the problem of involuntary singleness will
persist. Our churches need to teach that in relationships, as in other areas of life, God wants an active
people of faith rather than a passive pity party; a
people who both actively pray for relationships and
actively help them to happen.

We the church need to ask ourselves whether our
failure actively to help our singles find partners is
negligent. We need to dust off our prejudices about
everything from centuries-old matchmaking to com-
puter dating agencies to look for the best ways of
increasing the number of eligibles our singles meet.
The churches which are going to attract single people
in the third millennium are those which feed their
social needs as well as their spiritual hunger. These
churches will hold both social and spiritual gatherings specifically for their singles, aimed at maturing
them before God and giving them the opportunity to
form the friendships and marriages that they desire
and which delight God. My prediction is that such

magnet churches will not just attract singles, they will retain them as they form relationships, marriages and families.

Those churches which persist in neglecting their singles will see a perpetually revolving door. Their hard-won gains of evangelism will rapidly run off to other churches – or back to the world. The involuntary singles who remain in such churches will do so despite their churches' failure to care about their desire to marry, not because of it.

So that is the choice for our churches: either grow into vibrant communities in which young people meet, marry, produce offspring and grow old, or remain ambivalent about your unhappy backsliding singles, congregations which cannot see that church growth is about much more than just the Great Commission. For the missing link in our church growth strategies is a response to the crisis of involuntary singleness.

If I could help your church think through a response to singleness, then get in touch with me through the publisher, or e-mail me at iangregory@easynet.co.uk.